Benefits Information Guide

London: HMSO

About The Benefits Information Guide

The 1996 Benefits Information Guide has been revised and updated by the Benefits Agency Press & Publicity Office. The Guide has been available to Benefits Agency staff for a number of years. It has been so well received by staff that it has been made available to the public. This is the second year that it has been published by HMSO.

The Guide is intended to be an aid to the range of benefits and allied provisions available under Social Security legislation in the United Kingdom *.

The Guide is arranged under groups of specific benefits under a general heading, eg. information about Invalid Care Allowance is found in the section titled Sick and Disabled. All benefits are listed alphabetically in the index at the back of the Guide. Benefit rates shown are from April 1996 unless otherwise stated.

We are grateful for the help and advice we have received from various branches within the Benefits Agency and the Department of Social Security in the updating of the Benefits Information Guide.

We welcome your views about our publication. If you have any comments or suggestions, please send them to:

> Press & Publicity
> Benefits Agency (1st Floor)
> Sentinel House
> 16-22 Sutton Court Road
> Sutton
> Surrey SM1 4SX

* **The information in this Guide is for general advice and information only. It should not be treated as a complete or authoritative statement of the law.**

General advice and information can also be obtained from:
Freeline Social Security on **0800 666 555**.

Contents

Page

Contents

Contents

Contents

Contents

Section 1 Contents

Page

Sick and Disabled

Section
1

Attendance Allowance

Introduction

Leaflet DS702

Tax free non-contributory

AA Helpline: 0345 123456 (local call rate)

Conditions

Medical rules

Must normally have needed help for 6 months.

By day

Frequent attention throughout the day in connection with bodily functions or continual supervision throughout the day in order to avoid substantial danger to himself or others.

By night

Prolonged or repeated attention during the night in connection with bodily functions or continual supervision throughout the night in order to avoid substantial danger to himself or others.

These rules mean that someone could get Attendance Allowance (AA) if, for example, they need a lot of help to:

*   move around the house

*   eat or drink

*   use the toilet

*   wash, bath, dress or undress, shave

*   use a kidney machine

*   get in and out of bed

An examination by a doctor may be required.

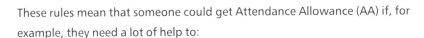

Sick and Disabled

April 1996

Benefits Information
Guide

Residence

In order to qualify for AA a person must satisfy both residence and presence conditions.

He must be:

(i)   Ordinarily resident in Great Britain - not the UK

(ii)   In Great Britain at the time of the claim

(iii)   Have been living in Great Britain or another EC country with worker status for a period or periods amounting to 26 weeks in the 12 months immediately preceding the claim

(iv)   Not be exempt from paying UK Income Tax

(v)   Must not have a condition or limitation on the right to reside in Great Britain

Persons living in the Isle of Man or Northern Ireland do **not** satisfy the residence conditions for payment but reciprocal arrangements do apply and a person who previously resided in the IOM or NI can be deemed to have satisfied the residence conditions if he was there in the 12 months preceding the claim.

Age

Over age 65 with no upper age limit. If under 65 years old when the incapacity began and before the 66th birthday at the date of claim, claim DLA.

Special Rules for terminally ill

Expected to live for less than 6 months

Must be living in Great Britain

Residence rules not applicable, except for point (v) under residence

When to claim

A claim for Attendance Allowance should be made immediately if claiming under the special rules otherwise a claim should be made if help has been needed for at least 3 months. If claiming under the special rules it is not necessary to complete section 2 of claim form DS2/DS2A. Form DS1500 completed by a doctor should be submitted to support the claim.

If DLA(mobility) is in payment, then if needed, DLA(care) should be claimed whatever the customer's age.

Request form for AA claim pack is contained in leaflet DS702.

Payment

There are two rates of Attendance Allowance:

- Higher rate £48.50 (If day and night conditions satisfied)
- Lower rate £32.40 (If day or night conditions satisfied)

Payment is made either by:-

- Order book cashable weekly or
- Credit transfer at 4 weekly intervals into a bank, building society, Girobank current account or National Savings Bank Investment Account

Attendance Allowance can not be paid to a person living in accommodation funded or helped by public money eg:

- Local Authority run homes
- Private/voluntary homes where costs are paid by the Local Authority

Passport

- Christmas Bonus
- Invalid Care Allowance

Sick and Disabled

Constant Attendance Allowance

Introduction

Leaflet NI 6

Tax free non-contributory.

Payable to persons in need of constant attention as a result of an industrial accident or industrial disease.

Conditions

- Disablement Benefit is in payment at 100%; or
- Disablement Benefit is paid at less than 100% but payment for disablement is being received from:

    - the Workmen's Compensation Act

    - the Pneumoconiosis, Byssinosis and Miscellaneous Diseases Benefit Scheme

    - the war pension scheme

    - injury pension under Police Pension Act or Fire Brigade Act

and these bring the total disablement to at least 100%.

Proof is required that daily attendance is needed and likely to be needed for a prolonged period.

When to claim

If industrial disablement is assessed at 95% or more the need for Constant Attendance Allowance (CAA) is automatically considered at the time of the medical examination.

A claim is required if a person who is in receipt of IIDB at the 100% rate (1) has initially had CAA disallowed or (2) then later discovers they need constant attendance because their circumstances have changed.

Sick and Disabled

Claim form BI 104 is available from local Benefits Agency offices.

Rate

	April 95	April 96
Part time	£19.10	£19.85
Normal maximum	£38.20	£39.70
Intermediate	£57.30	£59.55
Exceptional	£76.40	£79.40

Payment - by order book and combined with Disablement Benefit.

Passport

- Christmas Bonus

- Invalid Care Allowance

- Home Responsibilities Protection.

Overlap

Care Component of Disability Living Allowance and Attendance Allowance is reduced by the amount of any Constant Attendance Allowance.

If Attendance Allowance is awarded at a higher rate the balance may be payable.

Disregarded for Income Support purposes except for residents in nursing homes or residential care homes.

Disability Living Allowance

Introduction

Leaflet DS 704

Tax free non-contributory

DLA Helpline: 0345 123456 (local call rate)

Disability Living Allowance (DLA) replaced and extended the help given by Attendance Allowance and Mobility Allowance for people disabled before age 65. DLA (care) can be claimed from the age of three months and DLA (mobility) from age five. The criteria to receive benefit must be satisfied prior to age 65, and a claim for DLA must be submitted prior to the 66th birthday.

Attendance Allowance remains for people disabled after age 65.

Care component

The care component of DLA is for people who need help with personal care. There are 3 rates depending on the amount of care a person needs:

- the *higher* rate will be paid if a person needs help both day and night.

- the *middle* rate, if a person needs frequent help during the day or prolonged or repeated during the night.

- the *lower* rate, if a person needs help during a significant part of the day (but less help than for the middle rate) or if over age 16 and needs help to prepare a cooked main meal.

People who are terminally ill may automatically qualify for the highest rate of the care component even if no help is needed.

The criteria for the top two rates are the same as for the current higher and lower rates of Attendance Allowance.

Mobility component

The mobility component, for people aged 5 or over, is payable at two rates.

The *higher* rate is payable if a person is:

- virtually unable to walk; or

- has had both legs amputated at or above the ankle, or was born without legs or feet; or

- is both deaf and blind; or

- is severely mentally impaired with severe behavioural problems.

The *lower* rate is payable if a person can walk but needs someone with them to make sure that they are safe or to help them to find their way around.

Residence rule

In order to qualify for DLA a person must satisfy both residence and presence conditions.

He must be:

(i)   Ordinarily resident in Great Britain - not the UK

(ii)   In Great Britain at the time of the claim

(iii)   Have been living in Great Britain or another EC country with worker status for a period or periods amounting to 26 weeks in the 12 months immediately preceding the claim

(iv)   Not be exempt from paying UK Income Tax

(v)   Must not have a condition or limitation on the right to reside in Great Britain

Persons living in the Isle of Man or Northern Ireland do **not** satisfy the residence conditions for payment but reciprocal arrangements do apply and a person who previously resided in the IOM or NI can be deemed to have satisfied the residence conditions if he was resident there in the 12 months preceding the claim.

Qualifying period

There is a 3-months qualifying period for both components of DLA.

The need for help must be expected to last for 6 months.

Once awarded, DLA will continue to be paid irrespective of age, provided the criteria continue to be met.

Rates

Care Component

April 1995		**April 1996**	
Higher	£45.70	Higher	£46.70
Middle	£30.55	Middle	£31.20
Lower	£12.15	Lower	£12.40

Mobility Component

April 1995		**April 1996**	
Higher	£31.95	Higher	£32.65
Lower	£12.15	Lower	£12.40

Special rules for terminally ill

Expected to live for less than 6 months. Must be living in Great Britain, but the residence rule is not applicable, except for point (v) under residence.

Claim forms

Claim form DLA1/DLA1A.

If either DLA care or mobility components are already in payment a form DLA 434 should be used.

Sick and Disabled

Payment

If another Social Security benefit is in payment, DLA will normally be combined with that. Otherwise it is paid 4-weekly either by order book or into a bank, building society, National Girobank Current Account or a National Savings Bank Investment Account.

Passport

Any rate of DLA satisfies the:

- Disability Working Allowance (DWA) disability test

- Christmas Bonus

- Income Support availability exemption for students

- Income Support entitlement to Disability premium, Higher pensioner premium, Disabled premium

Higher and middle rate care component satisfies the:

- Severe Disablement Allowance 80% disability test

- Invalid Care Allowance test

Higher rate mobility component satisfies the:

- Exemption from road tax (DLA 403)

- Orange badge scheme (Social Services)

- Motability if customer is awarded higher rate DLA (mobility) for a period longer than the period of the motability agreement

Invalid Care Allowance

Introduction

Leaflet DS 700

Taxable non-contributory

ICA Helpline: 01253 856123

Invalid Care Allowance (ICA) is payable to someone caring for a severely disabled person. The disabled person must be in receipt of either Attendance Allowance or Constant Attendance Allowance, or the higher or middle rate of the care component of Disability Living Allowance.

Conditions

The carer must satisfy the following conditions:

*   Be caring for the disabled person for at least 35 hours a week

*   Be under age 65 at the time of claim. Once benefit is awarded it can continue to be paid over age 65 regardless of certain main entitlement conditions and no other NI benefit is in payment

*   Not be earning more than £50 per week (April 1996) after allowable expenses

*   Not be in full-time education

*   Be living in Great Britain and have done so for 6 out of the last 12 months (special rules apply for EC state members and HM Forces and their families)

When to claim

Immediately the carer satisfies the above conditions. The carer should also claim if the disabled person is waiting to hear the result of an AA/DLA claim. Backdating is possible up to 12 months.

The claim form is attached to leaflet DS 700.

Sick and Disabled

Payment

	April 1995	April 1996
Customer	£35.25	£36.60
Adult dependant	£21.10	£21.90
Eldest child	£ 9.85	£ 9.90
Each subsequent child	£11.05	£11.15

Dependants addition

To claim child dependency addition the partner must have earnings of less than:

First child	£130.00
For each additional child	£ 17.00

Payment

Payment is made by order book cashable weekly, in advance. ICA cannot be paid into a bank or building society account.

Passport

Christmas Bonus.

Class 1 credits awarded.

Carer Premium for those in receipt of Income Support and Housing Benefit providing ICA in payment (or underlying entitlement to ICA).

Overlap

ICA overlaps with most other Social Security Benefits. Only one ICA payable per disabled person.

Notes

Claims for ICA before 1 June 1992 can, in certain circumstances, continue to be paid if the person moves to another EC country.

Severe Disablement Allowance

Introduction

Leaflet NI 252 (Claim form attached)

Tax free non-contributory

7 days benefit from 13.4.95

Severe Disablement Allowance (SDA) is a benefit for customers who have not paid sufficient contributions to qualify for Incapacity Benefit.

Conditions

Medical

Must be:

- '80% disabled' unless incapacity started before aged 20. '80% disabled' is deemed if any of the following are in payment:
    - DLA mobility component higher rate
    - DLA care component at the two higher rates
    - War Pensions, Mobility Supplement or Industrial Injuries, Disablement Benefit at 80% plus: or

- registered blind or partially sighted; or

- receiving invalid car or private car allowance from Social Security; or

- receives a vaccine damage payment.

Must have been incapable of work for 28 weeks.

Must be submitting doctor's statements.

If not deemed 80% disabled a medical examination will be necessary. The handicap can be either physical or mental.

If qualifying period ended on or after 12 April 1995, the customer will have to satisfy the All Work Test.

Sick and Disabled

Residence

Must have been in Great Britain for at least 26 weeks of the 52 weeks immediately preceding date of claim.

Presence in another EC country may count towards this rule.

Age

Age 16 or over and under 65 when first qualifying for benefit.

Under 19s can only get SDA if their education is for less than 21 hours a week. Hours of tuition which are unsuitable for someone of the same age who does not have a physical or mental disability are ignored.

Payment

New claims for SDA will be paid fortnightly in arrears by girocheque or order book cashable at the Post Office or 4/13 weekly in arrears by ACT.

	April 1995	April 1996
Customer	£35.55	£36.95
Adult dependant	£21.15	£21.95
Eldest child	£ 9.85	£9.90
Each subsequent child	£11.05	£11.15

Adult dependency addition will be awarded if entitlement to child/dependency addition exists.

Other benefits

Cannot be paid with other NI benefits and is taken fully into account for Income Support.

Passport

Christmas Bonus.

Class 1 credits awarded (but only count for RP purposes).

Therapeutic work

Subject to the agreement of their doctor and the Benefits Agency, a customer may earn up to £45.50 (April 1996) a week working for less than 16 hours which will be of benefit to their health. This will also apply to voluntary work.

Notes

From 3 December 1990 age related additions are paid on top of SDA.

	April 1995	April 1996
Under 40	£12.40	£12.90
40-49	£ 7.80	£ 8.10
50-59	£ 3.90	£ 4.05

From 13/4/95 Incapacity Benefit rules apply to therapeutic earnings and the All Work Test.

Sick and Disabled

Exceptionally Severe Disablement Allowance

Introduction

Leaflet NI 6

Tax free

An extra allowance for those in receipt of Constant Attendance Allowance at the intermediate or exceptional rates.

Conditions

Receipt of Constant Attendance Allowance at the intermediate or exceptional rate.

Need for attendance is likely to be permanent.

When to claim

Automatic consideration is given to this benefit at the same time Constant Attendance Allowance is claimed.

Rate

	April 1995	April 1996
	£37.40	£38.20

Overlaps

Does not overlap with any other benefit.

Statutory Sick Pay

Introduction

Leaflets:

*   Customer   NI 245

*   Employer   CA 30

Taxable

Statutory Sick Pay (SSP) is payable to employees under pension age whose average earnings are at least the NI weekly lower earnings limit (£61.00 from April 1996).

Conditions

*   Must be employed under a contract of employment (Class 1) and have actually started work for the employer concerned.

*   Must be in the EC.

*   Married women with reduced liability are entitled.

*   Not affected by period in hospital.

*   Must be sick for more than 3 days.

Not entitled if:

*   Self-employed or unemployed (claim Incapacity Benefit).

*   Under 16 or over pension age (for woman with a period of incapacity for work beginning on or after 6 April 1994, pension age will be 65).

*   The Contract of Service is for 3 months or less.

*   Within the maternity pay period.

*   Claimed Incapacity Benefit/Sickness Benefit/Maternity Allowance (or under certain circumstances Unemployment Benefit) within the last 8 weeks.

Sick and Disabled

**Section
1**

- More than 28 weeks in one period of sickness.

- In legal custody.

- On strike.

Rate

Payable for 28 weeks, after which customer is transferred to Incapacity Benefit, if contributions conditions are satisfied.

Earnings £61.00 or more   SSP payable = £54.55

Earnings below £61.00   SSP payable = Nil

Payments are subject to tax and NI contributions.

Forms

SSPI   is issued by employer after 23 weeks or when liability to pay SSP ends or if the employee is not entitled to SSP.

Other benefits

Affects most other NI benefits except Widows Benefit

Incapacity Benefit

Introduction

Leaflet IB 201 Transitional Information

  IB 202 Incapacity Benefit

  IB 203 Getting back to work

Contributory

Two highest rates taxable

7 day benefit (IB replaced SB & IVB from April 1995)

Conditions

Medical

Claims should be submitted on Form SC1 (self-certificate) for claims of 4 to 7 days and a doctor's statement for subsequent periods. Claims must be made within one month of start of the incapacity, unless there is a good reason for delay.

Age

Customers must be under 60 (for Women)/65 (for Men).

First Contributions Condition

The first contribution condition is satisfied if in any tax year:

1 A customer has paid contributions of a relevant class

2 The contributions have been paid (or can be treated as being paid) before the day for which benefit is claimed; and

3 The earnings factor from those contributions is not less than 25 x the Lower Earnings Limit (LEL) for the year in which they were paid.

Special rules apply if the customer is a widow/recently divorced (woman) where the Period of Interruption of Employment (PIE) started before 28 May 1989/ recently finished full-time education.

Sick and Disabled

Section
1

Second Contribution Condition

For PIEs beginning on or after 2 October 1988 or claims beginning on or after 2 October 1989 irrespective of whether the claim links with an earlier PIE, the second contribution condition is satisfied if the:

1   Customer has paid or been credited with contributions of a relevant class or

2   has been credited with earnings and the earnings factor in each of those years must not be less than 50 x LEL for that year

Payment

No payment is made for the first 3 days of incapacity unless it is within 8 weeks of a previous claim to Incapacity Benefit (IB).

Periods of less than 4 consecutive days are not normally paid unless the customer is undergoing a course of dialysis, radiotherapy, chemotherapy, plasmapheresis or total parenteral nutrition for gross impairment of enteric function.

Rates

There are three rates of Incapacity Benefit :

*   Short term Incapacity Benefit lower rate, payable for first 28 weeks of incapacity

*   Short term Incapacity Benefit higher rate, payable for weeks 29-52 of incapacity (higher rate payable to those over pension age under transitional protection arrangement)

*   Long term Incapacity Benefit, payable from week 53 of incapacity. (Terminally ill and higher rate care DLA recipients are paid long term rate at week 29 of incapacity)

April 1996

Benefits Information
Guide

Short Term Incapacity Benefit   April 1996

Weeks 0 - 52	Lower Rate	£46.15
Weeks 29 - 52	Higher Rate	£54.55
Weeks 0 - 52	Over Pension Age	£58.65

Long Term Incapacity Benefit

Week 53 onwards	£61.15

Age Additions (paid with LTIB only)

Incapacity began before age 35	£12.90
Incapacity began between 35 - 44	£ 6.45

Invalidity Allowance (Transitional Protec.. on)

Higher rate	£12.90
Middle rate	£ 8.10
Lower rate	£ 4.05

Additional Pension (Transitional Protection)

Frozen at April 1994 rates, not uprated annually, and not available to new customers.

Note: Customers who are over pension age and getting their Additional Pension will have their AP uprated.

Adult dependency increase may be payable for a wife/husband/partner, subject to the length of time customer has been on IB and the dependant's income, age and if they are responsible for any children.

Extra benefit can sometimes be paid for dependant children.

Adult Dependency Increase

Short term IB	£28.55
Short term IB (over pension age)	£35.15
Long term IB	£36.60

Most claims to IB will be paid fortnightly in arrears by giro or order book, or 2, 4 or 13 weekly in arrears by ACT. (Form BF1009).

Some IB customers can request weekly payments on the grounds of hardship.

Sick and Disabled

Section
1

Passport

Gives eligibility to Class 1 credits

Christmas Bonus (available with LTIB)

Linking

Incapacity claims separated by more than eight weeks, even if UB is paid continuously between the two claims, will not link. Waiting days will be imposed on these non-linking IB claims.

Claims to an Incapacity benefit will only link if separated by a period of 8 weeks or less, unless special linking rules apply, ie DWA/Training.

Industrial Accident and Prescribed Disease

From 13.4.95 all customers claiming as a result of the above will have to satisfy the normal contribution conditions in order to qualify for IB.

Customers are still entitled to make a claim for Industrial Disablement Benefit.

Therapeutic Work

Subject to the agreement of their doctor and the Benefits Agency, a customer may earn up to £45.50 per week doing work for less than 16 hours which will be of benefit to their health (this limit on hours also applies to voluntary work). However, the 16 hour rule does not apply to work which is part of a medically supervised treatment programme as an in/regular out patient of a hospital or work done in a sheltered workshop.

Income Tax

From 13.4.95 Incapacity Benefit is classed as earned income for income tax purposes. All customers will require a tax code.

The taxable rates of IB are the short-term higher rate and the long-term rate and also taxable are the adult dependency increase and incapacity age addition.

Previous IVB customers will not be liable for tax unless there is a break in the claim of more than 8 weeks.

A P60 will be issued to all customers in receipt of taxable IB with details of tax paid on the previous year.

A P45 will be issued automatically when the claim ends and the account is closed.

Incapacity test

The test of incapacity for work will relate to the customer's ability to perform:

- their own occupation for the first 28 weeks ('own occupation'' test)

- any work from the 29th week (''all work'' test)

Own Occupation test

If the customer had a job for at least 8 of the 21 weeks prior to the start of their incapacity, the incapacity will only be considered in relation to their normal occupation.

Customers who have not had a job for 8 out of the last 21 weeks will be subject to the ''all work'' test immediately.

All Work test

Customers will be subject to the ''all work'' test:

- from the 29th week of incapacity if the customer satisfies the condition for their ''own occupation'' test, or

- immediately if the customer does not satisfy the condition for the ''own occupation'' test

The ''all work'' test will usually start with the issue of a questionnaire which is completed by the customer. The questionnaire consists of questions about the customer's ability to perform certain tasks, eg: How long can you stand unassisted?

Sick and Disabled

April 1996

Benefits Information
Guide

The customer will tick the relevant box from the options given. There is space provided after each set of questions for the customer to put additional information relating to their incapacity.

The customer should obtain a form "Med 4" from their doctor and enclose this with the questionnaire when the return it.

The questionnaire, which is the customer's view of how their incapacity affects them will, in most cases, be referred to BA Medical Services (BAMS) for assessment. The information given by the customer on the questionnaire is used when making the decision on incapacity.

The test will be applied to all customers on IB, new claims to SDA, previous IVB customers (at April 95) existing SDA customers, and credits only cases.

Cases that were No Further Control Action (NFCA) or No Need to Refer Again (NNRA) will also have the test applied to them from April 96 onwards.

The following customers will **not** be subject to the "all work" test:

- Previous IVB customers who were aged 58 or over on 13.4.95 and had been in receipt of IVB since 1.12.93, excluding any breaks of 8 weeks or less.

- Customers in receipt of highest rate Disability Living Allowance (DLA) Care Component.

- Customers who have certain specified incapacities.

- Customers who are terminally ill, ie expected to live 6 months or less.

There are special provisions for customers who are in hospital, pregnant or abroad.

Medical certificates will still be required until the "all work" test action is completed.

Industrial Injuries Disablement Benefit

Introduction

Leaflet NI 6

Tax free.

Industrial Accidents

Conditions

- Must be employed by an employer who pays them wages or a salary; and

- the injury is a result of an accident at work which happened after 4 July 1948, and the accident happened in Great Britain; or

- a member state of the European Community; or

- in a country with a reciprocal agreement covering industrial injuries; or

- anywhere abroad if payment of Class 1 contributions or special Class 2 contributions for volunteer development workers are being made.

Reporting Accidents

Any accident arising out of and in the course of employed earners employment should be reported to the employer immediately and the details entered either in an accident book or recorded by electronic means.

An Adjudication Officer will give a decision on whether an accident at work was an Industrial Accident on receipt of form BI 95 from the employee.

Industrial Diseases

- Must have one of the industrial diseases or a condition resulting from one of these diseases listed in leaflet NI 2; and

- must have been doing a job at some time in the type of work listed for the disease; and

- the disease is a result of that job.

Who can claim Disablement Benefit? - see "conditions" and:

- There must be some loss of physical or mental faculty as a result of the accident or disease.

- Disablement Benefit is not paid until 15 weeks (90 days excluding Sundays) after the date of accident or date of onset of the disease.

- A decision as to the percentage of disablement is made by a medical board.

- Awards of 14% - 19% are rounded up to 20% and a weekly pension is paid.

- Benefit will not be paid if the award is less than 14% unless there are other disablement assessments for other industrial accidents or diseases which cover a common period and when added together total 14% or more.

- People suffering from pneumoconiosis, byssinosis or diffuse mesothelioma will receive benefit even if the disablement is assessed at less than 14%.

When to claim

- Claim can be made immediately after the onset of disease but see above regarding first date of payment.

- Claim after being disabled by an accident for 9 weeks but see above regarding first date of payment.

- Claim forms are available from local Social Security offices.

- Accidents	Form BI 100A
- Pneumoconiosis & Byssinosis	Form BI 100 (Pn)
- Deafness because of your job	Form BI 100 (OD)
- Asthma because of your job	Form BI 100 (OA)
- Other Diseases	Form BI 100B
- Chronic Bronchitis and/or Emphysema	Form BI 100C

Payment

Rates:

Over 18 years or under 18 years if entitled to dependency benefits

		April 95	April 96
Disablement	100%	£95.30	£99.00
Disablement	90%	£85.77	£89.10
Disablement	80%	£76.24	£79.20
Disablement	70%	£66.71	£69.30
Disablement	60%	£57.18	£59.40
Disablement	50%	£47.65	£49.50
Disablement	40%	£38.12	£39.60
Disablement	30%	£28.59	£29.70
Disablement	20%	£19.06	£19.80

Different amounts apply to those under 18 without dependants. Payment is made by order book, and can be paid whether or not the person has returned to work and irrespective of their earnings.

ACT not available at present.

Maximum life gratuity (lump sum)

April 95	April 96
£6,330	£6,580

Transitional arrangements

For accidents and prescribed industrial diseases contracted before 6 April 1983 benefit may be payable from the date of first disablement rather than waiting 90 days.

Overlaps

Disablement Benefit is paid on top of any other NI benefit, eg: Incapacity Benefit or Retirement Pension. It can also be paid as well as SSP.

Disablement Benefit is paid in addition to a War Disablement Pension or Income Support or both. Disablement Benefit may however affect the amount of War Pension or Income Support payable.

Disablement Benefit may also affect the amount of any other income related benefits in payment such as Housing Benefit, Council Tax Benefits etc.

If a person suffers from more than one accident his total benefit payable cannot exceed 100% (excluding REA).

Reduced Earnings Allowance

Introduction

Leaflet NI 6

Tax free

Until 1/10/ 90 Reduced Earnings Allowance (REA) was available to people who, because of their disablement due to an industrial accident or prescribed disease, were unable to return to their regular occupation or to do work of an equivalent standard. Those who suffered accidents or contracted a prescribed disease before the above date will be treated under old rules and all REA entitlements acquired up to that time will be preserved and subject to uprating as now providing there is a continuous period of entitlement. For accidents occurring or prescribed diseases starting after 1/10/90 REA cannot be paid.

When to claim

A claim should be made immediately the conditions for REA are met.

Claim form BI103 available from the local Benefits Agency office.

Sick and Disabled

Payment

Amount payable is the difference between the current earning capacity and what would have been earned from previous regular occupation.

Maximum amount £39.60 per week (April 1996).

REA can be paid on top of Disablement Benefit as long as they have not stopped working or have been treated as not having given up working.

It can only be considered if the relevant degree of Industrial Disablement is assessed at 1% or more.

Disability Benefit is only paid if the degree of disablement is assessed at 14% or more.

From 1/10/89 for people who attain pension age and give up regular employment on or after 10 April 1989 REA will stop and will be replaced by Retirement Allowance. They will not have to claim Retirement Allowance as this is converted automatically.

Customers who retired before 10/4/89 had their REA frozen.

Imprisonment, detention in legal custody or absence abroad can affect entitlement.

Retirement Allowance

Introduction

Reduced Earnings Allowance (REA)

Customers who retired or are deemed retired for NI purposes on or after 10/4/89 will have their allowance replaced by Retirement Allowance (RA).

No Claim Necessary

Payment

Provided their REA was £2 per week or more, the rate will be the lesser of:

1.   25% of the weekly REA that the customer was entitled to the day before he retired; or

2.   10% of the maximum rate of disablement pension - £9.90 (April 96).

If the total amount of REA to which a customer is entitled immediately before he retires is less than £2 per week there will be no title to RA.

RA will be awarded for life and paid on a Wednesday as with REA and Disablement Benefit. It can be paid even when the basic Disablement Benefit expires or becomes less than 1%.

War Disablement Pension

Introduction

Leaflets:

*   WPA 1   Notes about War Pensions

*   WPA 2   Notes for people getting a War Pension

*   WPA 3   Notes for people getting a War Pension (Overseas)

*   WPA 4   Notes for people not getting a War Pension

*   WPA 5   Notes for people not getting a War Pension (Overseas)

*   WPA 8   Can I claim?

*   WPA 9   Rates of War Pensions

Tax free

War Pensions Helpline: 01253 858858

War Disablement Pension (WDP) may be payable to those who

*   served in HM armed forces and whose disablement is due to an injury which is attributable to or aggravated by service or

*   were civilians or Civil Defence Volunteers and whose disablement was caused by a war injury or war service injury in the 1939-1945 war or (**Note** claims by civilians for War Disablement Pensions are now outside the time limit. Claims may still be considered if independent corroborative evidence to support the claim can be provided) or

*   were merchant seamen, coastguards or members of the Naval Auxiliary Service whose disablement is directly attributable to a qualifying injury received during time of war or to the effects of detention by the enemy or

*   were members of the Polish Forces under British Command or in the Polish Resettlement Forces whose disablement is due to an injury which is attributable to or aggravated by that service or

- were members of the Home Guard whose disablement is due to an injury which is attributable to or aggravated by service

How to claim

Write to the following address:

> War Pensions Agency
> Norcross
> BLACKPOOL
> Lancashire   FY5 3WP

Payment

If the disability (assessed by a doctor) is less than 20%, a lump sum payment can be awarded. However, for claims made on or after 7 January 1993 in respect of the condition **noise induced sensorineural hearing loss**, no payment is made where the assessment is less than 20%.

For disabilities assessed at 20% or above, a pension is awarded.

See leaflet WPA 9 for current rates.

Allowances

War Disablement Pensioners may be entitled to the following allowances:

- Allowance for Lowered Standard of Occupation
- Unemployability Supplement
- Constant Attendance Allowance
- Comforts Allowance
- Exceptionally Severe Disablement Allowance
- Severe Disablement Occupational Allowance
- Clothing Allowance

- Age Allowance

- Mobility Supplement

- Treatment Allowance

Note: some of the above allowances may overlap with other Social Security benefits.

Medical treatment

The War Pensions Agency can ask for a measure of priority if a war pensioner needs treatment for his/her pensioned disablement.

All requests for priority treatment should be addressed in the first instance to:

War Pensions Agency (Treatment Group),
Norcross, Blackpool, FY5 3WP.

Prescriptions are free if the treatment is for the pensionable disablement.

Notes

Disregard of £10 per week on basic WDP applied to Income Support, Housing benefit/Council Tax benefit and Family Credit, but some local authorities may disregard more than £10 on claims for Housing benefit/Council Tax benefit.

Sick and Disabled

Vaccine Damage Payments

Introduction

Leaflet HB 3

Tax free

How to claim

Claims should be made before age 18 within 6 years of the date of vaccination or the date on which the disabled child reached 2 years of age.

Claim forms are available from:

> Vaccine Damage Payments Unit
> Palatine House
> Lancaster Road
> Preston PR1 1HB
> Tel: 01772 899693

Conditions

This is a one-off payment of £30,000 to people who are severely disabled as a result of either:

1. having been vaccinated against diphtheria, tetanus, whooping cough, tuberculosis, polio-myelitis, measles, rubella (German measles) mumps or Hib (haemophilus Influenzae type b); or

2. having become severely disabled as a result of a close personal contact with a person who has been vaccinated with an orally administered polio-myelitis vaccine; or

3. having become severely disabled because their mother was vaccinated whilst she was pregnant. In addition, the disabled person must be aged 2 or over and vaccinated in the UK or the Isle of Man.

The vaccination must have taken place before the customer's 18th birthday unless it was against polio-myelitis or rubella during an outbreak of that disease within the UK or Isle of Man. Vaccinations outside the UK are only considered if the disabled person or someone in his family were in the armed forces and the vaccination was given as part of the armed services medical facilities.

Disability Working Allowance

Introduction

Leaflet DS 703

Claim form DWA1

DWA Helpline: 01772 883300

Tax free non-contributory

Disability Working Allowance (DWA), is a benefit to help people with an illness or disability who are starting work or are already working.

Who can claim DWA

People aged 16 or over who satisfy all 3 of the following conditions may be able to get DWA.

Work

DWA is available to people who are starting paid work for 16 hours or more a week, or are already working 16 hours or more a week. This can be self-employed work or working for an employer. If the job is temporary it must be expected to last at least 5 weeks.

Since July 1995, a £10.30 (April 96) premium is available to people working 30 hours or more a week.

Disability

DWA is available to people who have an illness or disability which puts them at a disadvantage in getting a job. The definition of what constitutes a disability which puts a customer at a disadvantage is set out in regulations.

Qualifying benefits

To qualify for DWA a person must either be getting:

Disability Living Allowance

Attendance Allowance

War Disablement Pension with either Constant Attendance Allowance or a mobility supplement

Industrial Injuries Disablement Benefit with Constant Attendance Allowance

An invalid three wheeler <u>or</u>

Be getting or have been getting on at least one of the 56 days before the date of claim:

Incapacity Benefit (short term higher rate or long term rate)

Severe Disablement Allowance

Income Support with Disability Premium

Housing Benefit with Disability Premium

Council Tax Benefit with Disability Premium

How much

DWA is an income-related benefit. The amount of DWA depends on the make-up of the customer's family and their financial resources such as income and capital, with a tapered withdrawal of benefit as income rises.

Since April 1995 DWA claimants with a disabled child are awarded a Disabled Childs Allowance. In order to receive the DCA, the child must either be in receipt of DLA, registered blind, or have been taken off the blind register within the last 28 weeks.

Customers with a child under 11 years old will be able to offset up to £60.00 per week of child care costs against their earnings when claiming DWA/Family Credit, where couples are both working at least 16 hours a week or one is incapacitated and the other partner is working or are a lone parent. If the partner is incapacitated they have to be in receipt of one of the benefits which is a qualifying benefit for DWA.

Capital

People with more than £16,000 are not entitled to DWA. For people with capital between £3,000 and £16,000 a weekly income is assumed and taken into account in the calculation of DWA. Some forms of capital are ignored, such as the surrender value of a life insurance policy, annuity, compensation from personal injury held in trust, and the value of a person's home and their personal possessions.

Income

Income is all the money that is coming into the customer's household including earnings, other income and an assumed income from capital. Tax, national insurance contributions and half of any contributions to an occupational or personal pension are deducted from the earnings which are taken into account. Some Social Security Benefits are not taken into account in the calculation for DWA.

Disability

For first claims:

A simple declaration by the customer that they have a physical or mental disability which puts them at a disadvantage in getting a job will usually provide sufficient evidence of disability.

For second and subsequent claims:

Customers are given a list of functional disabilities which are likely to put them at a disadvantage in the labour market and are asked to indicate which apply to them. To 'pass' the test they have to have one or more of the specified disabilities. They are also asked to name a professional involved in their care who can provide confirmation of their assessment. People who are receiving DLA at a higher rate, or who were getting SDA before claiming DWA, are assumed to satisfy the disability test and will generally not need to complete a self assessment form.

Period of award

DWA is awarded for a fixed period of 26 weeks. Eight weeks before the award ends the customer is sent a form on which to make a renewal claim - renewal claims can be made within the period 6 weeks before and 2 weeks after the end of the DWA award. Payment is made in arrears on a Tuesday either direct to a bank account or by order book. If payment is made by ACT it is made 4 weekly in arrears. The final payment being for 2 weeks.

National Insurance (NI) Credits

Class 1 NI credits may be awarded to DWA customers whose earnings in any week fall below the lower earnings limit for paying NI contributions.

Reviews

All decisions about a DWA claim are taken by independent Adjudication Officers. A person dissatisfied with an Adjudication Officer's decision has the right to an informal review by a different Adjudication Officer.

Appeals

If a person remains unhappy following a review decision they have the right of appeal to a new independent Disability Appeal Tribunal. The Tribunal will have at least one person who is experienced in the needs of disabled people.

Linking

A person receiving DWA who was receiving Invalidity/Incapacity Benefit (short term higher rate or long term rate) or Severe Disablement Allowance before claiming DWA, whose attempt at work fails within 2 years, and who is incapable of work, will be eligible for the benefit they were receiving rather than for Incapacity Benefit. In order for the 2 year link to apply, customers need to be in receipt of DWA when they give up. This 'Linking Rule' is unique to DWA. The normal rule is that people who give up Invalidity/Incapacity Benefit or SDA can return to them only if they become incapable of work within 8 weeks, otherwise they have to re-serve a 28-week qualifying period.

Training for Work

Access to DWA has been extended to help those who have undertaken Training for Work.

This will apply if they start their Training for Work within 56 days of last receiving either Incapacity benefit (short term higher or long term rate) or SDA. When training ceases and they start work DWA must be claimed within 56 days of ceasing their training.

Passport

- Free NHS charges if savings are under £8,000.

- Gives eligibility to claim Social Fund Maternity Payments, Funeral Payments and Crisis Loans. If Housing Benefit and Council Tax benefit is claimed the £10.30 premium will be disregarded.

Examples

Single person working more than 16 hours per week bringing home £70 per week.

Maximum Allowance		£48.25
Applicable amount		£56.40
Calculation:		
Income		£70.00
Applicable amount		£56.40
	=	£13.60
£13.60 x 70%		£9.52
Maximum Allowance		£48.25
DWA	=	£38.73

Married couple, 2 children, one under 11, one between 11 and 15. Customer works more than 16 hours per week and brings home £85 per week.

Maximum Allowance	£106.80
Applicable amount	£ 75.20

Calculation:

Income			£ 85.00
Applicable amount			£ 75.20
		=	£ 9.80
£9.80 x 70%			£ 6.86
Maximum Allowance			£106.80
DWA		=	£ 99.94

Independent Living (1993) Fund

Introduction

The Independent Living (1993) Fund is a new trust set up to provide cash payments to severely disabled people. It is financed by the Government, but administered by seven independent trustees. The original Independent Living Fund was discontinued in March 1993 but existing clients continue to be dealt with.

The address of the Independent Living Fund is:

Independent Living Fund
PO Box 183
Nottingham
NR8 3RD
Tel: 0115 929427

Eligibility

An applicant to the Fund must meet all the following conditions:

- Be at least 16 and under 66 years of age.

- Receive the highest rate of the care component of Disability Living Allowance.

- Be at risk of entering residential care (or currently be in residential care and wish to leave and live independently).

- Be on Income Support or have an income above Income Support level which is less than the cost of the care needed.

- Have savings of less than £8,000.

Hospital Admission

Leaflet NI 9

How benefits are affected on admission to Hospital

Admission to hospital by customer or dependant must be notified immediately. Similar action should be taken on discharge.

The Benefits Agency should be notified when an in-patient is allowed home even for a few days - as this can affect the rate of benefit payable.

Main NI benefits

RP, over 80s pension, Widows Benefit, Widowed Mothers Allowance, Severe Disablement Allowance and Incapacity Benefit

The above benefits are reduced:

Immediately

None are reduced immediately unless the customer is living in a local authority home (not a council house) or has been in hospital for 6 weeks or more.

After 6 weeks

	April 1995	April 1996
With a dependant - benefit reduced by	£11.75	£12.25
Without a dependant - benefit reduced by	£23.50	£24.50

After 1 year

Benefit reduced to	£11.75	£12.25

If the customer has a dependant, benefit is reduced by a further £12.25, ie £24.50 in total.

Sick and Disabled

Linking

Individual spells of hospital in-patient treatment are added together and count towards the reduction if each spell is separated by less than 4 weeks out of hospital.

Resettlement benefit

Resettlement Benefit was abolished on 11 April 1988. Any entitlement to Resettlement Benefit accrued under old rules will be paid as a lump sum when the person is discharged from hospital.

Other benefits

DLA Care Component: withdrawn after 4 weeks.

DLA Mobility Component: continues in payment unless the customer is unable to use the allowance, ie in a coma.

Invalid Care Allowance: may cease immediately, but can continue up to 12 weeks depending on personal circumstances and those of the person cared for.

Statutory Sick Pay: paid by an employer and is not reduced.

Income Support: see Income Support Chart.

Income Support Chart - Hospital in-patients. Rates from April 1996

Downrating action - time in hospital. This applies whether it is the customer or the customer's dependant who goes into hospital.

Income Support

After 4 Weeks

Severe Disability Premium (SDP) is withdrawn. Entitlement to Disabled Child Premium (DCP), Disability Premium (DP), Higher Pensioner Premium (HPP) and Severe Disablement premium (SDP) should be reviewed when the person to whom the premium relates has been in hospital for more than 4 weeks. DLA/AA should be withdrawn when the person to whom it relates has been in hospital for more than 4 weeks. However, if the recipient is a member of a couple and the withdrawal of DLA/AA is only due to hospitalisation, then entitlement to the SDP will remain unchanged.

After 6 Weeks

Single person
Benefit is reduced to £15.30 plus some housing costs.

Couple, one in hospital
Benefit is reduced by £12.25

Couple, both in hospital
Benefit is reduced to £30.60 plus some housing costs.
If you have dependant children, you will still receive benefit for them and your family premium.

Lone Parent
Benefit is reduced to £15.30 plus any housing costs and any benefit for dependant children. You will still receive your family premium and your lone parent premium.

Sick and Disabled

Sick and Disabled

**Housing Benefit and
Council Tax Benefit**

If you got Income Support and it has now been stopped, your Housing Benefit and Council Tax Benefit will also stop unless you make a new claim to your local Council. Get a copy of leaflet RR1 'Help with Rent' to claim Housing Benefit and/or a copy of leaflet CTB 1 'Help with the Council Tax' to claim Council Tax Benefit. The leaflets can be obtained from a Social Security office or main post office. Send the coupon(s) to your local Council and they will send you the claim form(s). If you are not getting or stop getting Income Support, then Housing Benefit and Council Tax Benefit may be paid to you at a reduced rate. Contact your local Council for more information.

Income Support

After 12 Weeks
Allowances for Housing costs are reviewed after 12 weeks (and will be reviewed about every 3 months).

Dependants
The amount you get for a dependant in hospital is £12.25 after they have been in hospital for 12 weeks.

After 1 Year
All Customers
The Hospital personal allowance rate of Income Support is reduced to £12.25. Less may be paid if the hospital authorities feel that you cannot make full use of this money.

Single Person
Housing costs are no longer paid.

Couple
Each will need to claim separately.

Lone Parent
If you are still responsible for your children, you can continue to get benefit for them and you will still get lone parent premium and family premium. If your children still live at home, you can go on getting help with housing costs.

Sick and Disabled

**Housing Benefit and
Council Tax Benefit**

**If you do not have a
partner or a dependant**
Housing Benefit will
normally stop.

**If you have a partner at
home**
He or she can claim
Housing Benefit instead
of you.

**If you have a
dependant**
Housing Benefit will
normally stop but the
dependant may be able
to claim. Ask your
Council.
Council Tax Benefit can
be paid for as long as
you have to pay the
charge. But if you are
permanently resident in
hospital, you may be
exempt from paying the
charge.
Contact your local
Council Tax Registration
Officer about this.
If you are exempted
from the charge but you
have a partner at home,
your partner can claim
Council Tax Benefit.

If your dependant goes into Hospital

Benefit - Retirement Pension, Over 80s Pension, Widows' Benefits, Invalid Care Allowance, Severe Disablement Allowance, Unemployability Supplement (with Industrial Injuries Disablement Benefit), Incapacity Benefit.

Immediately

If someone who looks after your child goes into hospital, dependency benefit for that person may stop.

After 6 weeks

Dependency benefit for husband or wife is usually reduced by £12.25 a week.

After 12 weeks

Benefit for a child stops unless you regularly spend money on things like small necessities, gifts and visits.

After 52 weeks

Dependency benefit for husband or wife is reduced to £12.25 a week.

Sick and Disabled

Section 2 Contents

Page

Maternity Payment from the Social Fund

Introduction

Leaflet FB8

Claim form SF100

Non-contributory tax free

Conditions

Customer or partner must be in receipt of Income Support, Family Credit or Disability Working Allowance.

Savings over £500 will be offset against the payment, £1000 if you or your partner are 60 or over.

Payment will be made where the pregnancy lasts to the 24th week even if a still-birth occurs.

When to claim

The claim must be made between the 11th week before expected week of confinement and 3 months after the actual date of confinement.

If the claim is made in respect of an adopted child, it must be made within 3 months of the adoption and when the child is not more than 1 year old.

Payment

By Girocheque.

Rate - £100.00 for each child.

The Maternity Payment is not recoverable from the customer and is not constrained by the local office Social Fund budget.

Statutory Maternity Pay

Introduction

Leaflet (Employer) CA 29

Leaflet (Employee) NI 17A

Non-contributory taxable

Paid by employers who claim back some of the money paid from NI payments sent to the Collectors of Taxes.

Conditions

- continuously employed by the same employer for at least 26 weeks up to and including her 'qualifying week' (QW). The QW is the 15th week before the Expected Week of Confinement (EWC)

- the employer should be given at least 21 days notice of the intention to stop work to have the baby. He may need the notice in writing

- average earnings must be at least the NI weekly lower earnings limit £61.00 per week from 6 April 1996

- still pregnant 11 weeks before EWC or confined by that time. Still births are paid for, providing the child is born not earlier than the 25th week of pregnancy

- no longer working

- payable even if there is no intention of returning to work

Payment

Statutory Maternity Pay (SMP) is paid for a maximum of 18 weeks commencing not earlier than 11 weeks before EWC and no later than the Sunday following the date baby was born. The customer can choose to continue at work right up until the baby's birth and still get the full 18 weeks benefit.

If the customer is absent from work for a pregnancy-related reason on or after the 6th week before the week the baby is due, the Maternity Pay Period will start automatically from either

- the Sunday of the week they are first absent if they have not worked or been entitled to Statutory Sick Pay from their employer that week, or

- the Sunday following the week they are first absent if they had worked or been entitled to Statutory Sick Pay from their employer that week.

There is no extra payment if the baby is born late or it is a multiple birth.

If someone satisfies the conditions for SMP with more than one employer they are entitled to SMP for each employer.

Rates

Higher rate

90% of average earnings. This is paid for the first 6 weeks of SMP.

Lower rate

£54.55 per week. Paid to customers for the balance of their SMP.

Payments received are subject to Tax and NI contributions.

Maternity Allowance can still be paid to people who are not entitled to SMP.

SMP is not a 'linking benefit'.

SMP overlaps with certain NI benefits.

April 1996

Benefits Information
Guide

Maternity Allowance

Introduction

Claim pack MA1

Leaflet NI17A

Leaflet FB8

Tax free contributory

If because of self-employment, unemployment, a recent change of jobs or for some other reason the customer is not entitled to Statutory Maternity Pay (SMP), a claim can be made for Maternity Allowance (MA).

Conditions

Must:

* still be pregnant 11 weeks before baby is due

* have stopped work

* not be entitled to SMP

* have worked and paid standard rate NI contributions as an employed or self-employed person for at least 26 out of the 66 weeks before the Expected Week of Confinement (EWC)

When to claim

The claim should be made as soon as possible after the beginning of the 14th week before the EWC.

Forms required are:

* MA1 - the claim pack

* SMP1 - if employed

* Mat B1 - Certificate of Expected Confinement

Payment rate

The rate payable depends on the employment status during the qualifying week (15th week before the EWC). A woman in employment but not entitled to SMP receives the higher rate of MA which is equivalent to the standard rate of SMP (£54.55). A woman who is self-employed or non-employed receives the lower rate of MA (£47.35). Entitlement is for a maximum of 18 weeks.

MA is normally payable:

- for a woman who is unemployed, from the 11th week before the expected week of confinement;

- for a woman who is employed or self-employed, from a week of her choosing, but not earlier than the 11th week before the expected week of confinement and no later than the Sunday following the date baby was born.

Entitlement to MA starts automatically however, if at an earlier stage the woman:

- gives birth; or

- following the beginning of the 6th week before the expected week of confinement, is absent from work for a pregnancy related reason.

Payment

Paid weekly by order book or by automatic credit transfer.

Incapacity Benefit 'in the alternative'

If there is no entitlement to SMP or MA, the customer may be able to get Incapacity Benefit for a period of 6 weeks before the EWC to 2 weeks after the actual Date of Confinement. The local Benefits Agency office will automatically look at the contribution conditions for Incapacity Benefit when disallowing an MA claim.

Child Benefit

Introduction

Leaflets:

- CH1   Child Benefit

- CH7   CHB for children aged 16 and over

- CH4   CHB children away from home

- CH4A Social Security and children in the care of a local authority

- CH5   CHB for people entering Britain

- CH6   CHB for people leaving Britain

- CH8   About Child Benefit

Tax free non-contributory

Conditions

Age

Payable for a child under 16, or aged 16, 17 or 18 and still studying full-time at school or college up to and including 'A' level standard.

Residence

Child or person claiming benefit must normally have lived in Great Britain for more than 26 weeks in the past 52 weeks. Special rules apply to certain groups:

- residence conditions - 26 weeks
- residence is waived if Class 1 or 2 NI is being paid and you intend to stay for more than 6 months
- parent from EC
- Western Europe
- Australia
- New Zealand

When to claim

As soon as child is born. Claim packs are available from Benefits Agency offices.

Can be backdated up to 26 weeks.

Payment rate

For eldest qualifying child   £10.80

For each other child   £8.80

Child Benefit payable 3 weeks in arrears, 1 week in advance (usually by order book) or by Automatic Credit Transfer (ACT) 4 weekly in arrears.

Arrangements can be made for benefit to be paid weekly (except Armed Forces) if:

- getting Income Support
- getting Family Credit
- a lone parent
- getting Disability Working Allowance
- on hardship grounds (contact local Benefits Agency office)

Note

Child Benefit continues to be paid for the period of the vacation after the term in which the child leaves school unless:

- they start full-time work of 24 hours or more each week

- they receive Income Support in their own right

- they start Youth Training (YT) scheme or a training course sponsored by an employer

Not payable if:

- child in care

- child in receipt of Severe Disablement Allowance or Income Support

- customer is a foster parent to a child boarded out by the local authority

- child on an advanced course of education, ie higher than 'A' level

- child on a Training Course sponsored by an employer or on a YT scheme

- child over 16, left school and is in full-time paid employment (24 hours or more)

- parent(s) are exempt from paying UK Income Tax, ie working

- for a foreign government or international organisation

- child married to a person who has left school

Priority

When more than one person claims, for example separated couples, the person who looks after the child usually receives Child Benefit.

Child Benefit extension period

Child Benefit can in certain circumstances be extended for a person under age 18 and not in full-time education.

This must be claimed for:

- summer leavers 16 weeks from the second Monday in September; or

- 12 weeks from the second Monday in January; or

- 12 weeks from the second Monday after Easter

The first available period following the end of the earlier award is used.

Must have registered for work or YT.

One Parent Benefit

Introduction

Leaflet CH11

Tax free non-contributory

One Parent Benefit (OPB) is available to people responsible for bringing up a child/children on their own.

Conditions

Customer must be in receipt of Child Benefit and either:

- single

- divorced

- widowed and not receiving extra money for child in Widows Benefit

- legally separated

- living apart (if married, must be separated for 13 weeks or more; for unmarried customers can be paid immediately upon permanent separation)

Not payable if:

- partner is in prison or hospital

- already in receipt of Guardians Allowance (prior to April 93only)

- an increase for a child is paid with:
    - Widowed Mothers Allowance
    - War Widows Pension
    - Invalid Care Allowance
    - Retirement Pension

Benefits which attract a dependency increase will find that increase is reduced by One Parent Benefit. Examples are:

- Income Support

- Unemployment Benefit - if over pension age

- Incapacity Benefit (but not Statutory Sick Pay)

- Severe Disablement Allowance

When to claim

As soon as the customer starts to bring up child on his/her own. But if recently separated from spouse the claim should be made shortly before the separation has lasted 13 weeks, or earlier if a divorce or separation with a Court Order comes through.

Complete form CH11A (contained in Leaflet CH11).

Payment rate

£6.30 paid with Child Benefit either:

- weekly by order book

- 4 weekly by order book

- 4 weekly direct into bank account or building society

Guardians Allowance

Introduction

Leaflet NI 14

Claim form BG 1

Tax free non-contributory

Conditions

The child must be qualifying child, ie:

- both parents must be dead; or

- if the child is illegitimate, mother dead and father not known; or

- parents divorced, one parent dead and other does not have custody, and was not paying voluntary maintenance for the child and was not liable; or

- if one parent is dead, other in prison for 5 years or more, or an indefinite period (allowance stops when parent released);
  NB Payment in these cases only commences once sentence is announced or

- one parent dead, whereabouts of other unknown

Must be entitled to Child Benefit for the child.

The child must live with customer or be maintained by customer at the rate of at least £11.15 per week (in addition to payments made to qualify for Child Benefit).

Residence conditions must be satisfied, by the deceased parent ie:

- one parent must have been born in UK; or

- after age 16, have spent a total of 52 weeks in any two year period in the UK

Orphaned child - no need for the customer to be the legal guardian.

Not paid..

- in respect of legally adopted child

- to local authority or voluntary organisation

If the relevant parents' death occurred before 6 April 1975 and parent was not insured under NI scheme.

When to claim

Claim within 6 months of entitlement.

In the case of a married couple living together the wife must make the claim.

Payment

Paid weekly by order book.

Eldest child	£ 9.90
Each subsequent child	£11.15

The rate of Guardians Allowance paid for a child will depend upon the actual rate of Child Benefit paid for that specific child eg if the guardian already has Child Benefit for an older child of her/his own the Guardians Allowance would automatically be paid at the subsequent child rate of £11.15.

Other benefits

Where there is entitlement to an increase in a Social Security Benefit for a child at a rate which does not exceed the rate of Guardians Allowance, then the increase in the other benefit is not payable.

With other increases, the other benefit is adjusted by reducing it by the rate of Guardians Allowance. The balance, if any, of the increase in the other benefit, together with Guardians Allowance, is payable.

Since April 1993 the payment of Guardians Allowance no longer affects entitlement to One Parent Benefit.

Family Credit

Introduction

Claim Pack FCl

FC47 Adviser briefing

NI 261 Guide to Family Credit

Tax free non-contributory

FC Helpline: 01253 500050

Family credit (FC) is available to parents (married/unmarried or lone parents) who are employed or self-employed, who work for 16 hours or more a week, who have at least one child living with them of school age and have no more than £8,000 in savings.

In two parent families, the woman must claim.

Conditions

The customer or partner must be working at least 16 hours a week and the job be expected to last for 5 weeks or more from the date of the claim.

A family must be responsible for at least one child under 16 (or under 19 in full-time education up to and including 'A' level standard) who is living with them as a family member.

The customer must normally be resident in Great Britain, with the partner 'ordinarily' resident in the UK.

Amount payable

The amount of FC payable is dependent on:

- number of hours worked

- number of children and their ages

- the level of family income and capital

- registered child minding fees payable (if any)

- the applicable amount

- the appropriate maximum credit (as laid down by Parliament)

- when the normal weekly income exceeds the applicable amount, the prescribed percentage (as laid down by Parliament) of the excess income

Earnings

Net earnings are calculated by deducting income tax, NI contributions and half of any superannuation due from the customer's or partner's wages/salary.

Disregards on income

All other income is taken fully into account except for:

- Child Benefit

- One Parent Benefit

- Guardian Allowance

- Maternity Allowance/Statutory Maternity Pay

- Housing Benefit

- Council Tax Benefit

- Personal Council Tax Transitional relief or reduction

- Attendance Allowance

- Disability Living Allowance

- Christmas Bonus

- Constant Attendance Allowance

The first £15 of maintenance payments are disregarded.

Payments made to a third party as part of maintenance settlement (ie ex-husband pays mortgage direct to building society) count as income for FC claim. The reason is that method of payment is purely one of convenience and the husband is effectively paying the wife.

Maintenance payments paid direct to a child are taken into account as part of customers income.

Income to dependant child from Trust Funds or covenants, etc are treated differently, ie if they exceed the child credit then no credit for the child is awarded and any balance is ignored.

The first £10 of the following is disregarded:

- Widow's Pension/War Widow's Pension/War Pension

- Student Loan

The first £20 of the following is disregarded:

- Charitable/voluntary payments

The first £5 of students covenant income is disregarded.

Income from boarders and sub-tenants follow the same disregard rules as for Income Support.

Capital

There is an upper capital limit of £8,000.

An income of £1 a week for each £250 (or part of £250) held in savings over £3,000 is assumed.

Applicable amount

The amount is £75.20.

Maximum credit

Adult Credit £46.45

Child Credits

- age 0 - 10 £11.75

- age 11 - 15 £19.45

- age 16 - 17 £24.15

- age 18 £33.80

A credit for a child will not be given if:

- a child has capital of more than £3,000 or

- a child has been in hospital or residential home for 12weeks at the time of claim (depends on illness and definition of regular contact) or

- a child's income exceeds maximum credit stipulated for him/her

The child will continue to be treated as a member of the family for all other purposes but will not receive a credit in the calculations.

Prescribed percentage = 70%

Set at 70% of the excess income over applicable amounts. The resulting figure is deducted from the maximum credit due and the balance paid as FC, unless the difference is less than 50p or the excess income exceeds the maximum credit in which case no FC is payable.

Calculation

If the family's net income is below the applicable amount, the amount of FC paid is the total of the Adult and Child credits due (maximum FC).

If the family's net income is above the applicable amount the following calculation can be used:

Maximum credit = A

Net Income = B

Applicable amount = C

$$\text{FC payable} = \frac{\text{A minus } [(B-C) \times 70]}{100}$$

Award

FC is normally paid for 6 months and will not usually be affected by changes in circumstances during an award period.

From July 1996, when FC is in payment for one child only and that child leaves full-time non-advanced eduacation, benefit will be withdrawn from that date. Child Benefit may still continue until the usual 'terminal' date.

Maternity and Child Benefits

Child care charges

Customers with a child under 11 years old can have up to £60.00 per week of certain child care costs offset against their earnings when claiming Family Credit.

It is available to couples where both are working or one is incapacitated and the other partner is working, or a lone parent, providing a registered child minder or nursery is used.

Payment

FC is paid either by:

- ACT 4 weekly in arrears

- by weekly order book

If the entitlement is £4.00 per week or less, the Family Credit due will be paid as a lump sum at the start of the award period.

For two parent families, the order book usually shows the mother as the payee with the partner as the alternative payee.

Other help available

People who get FC do not have to pay for the following for themselves or their children:

- NHS prescriptions

- NHS dental treatment

- NHS eye test

- travel to hospital for NHS treatment

They can also get help with the following:

- cost of glasses

- Social Fund payments (Maternity and funeral payments only)

Powdered milk is available for children under one at a reduced price.

Note

Customers working 30 hours or more per week receive an additional £10.30 premium.

To get full benefit from this, the premium is disregarded in any calculation for Housing Benefit/Council Tax Benefit.

Maternity and Child Benefits

Family Credit Ready Reckoner 1996/97

Income £	A	B	C	D	AA	AB	AC	AD
75.20	58.20	65.90	70.60	80.25	69.95	77.65	82.35	92.00
80.00	54.84	62.54	67.24	76.89	65.59	74.29	78.99	88.64
85.00	51.34	59.04	63.74	73.39	63.09	70.79	75.49	85.14
90.00	47.84	55.54	60.24	69.89	59.59	67.29	71.99	81.64
95.00	44.34	52.04	56.74	66.39	56.09	63.79	68.49	78.14
100.00	40.84	48.54	53.24	62.89	52.59	60.29	64.99	74.64
105.00	37.34	45.04	49.74	59.39	49.09	56.79	61.49	71.14
110.00	33.84	41.54	46.24	55.89	45.59	53.29	57.99	67.64
115.00	30.34	38.04	42.74	52.39	42.09	49.79	54.49	64.14
120.00	26.84	34.54	39.24	48.89	38.59	46.29	50.99	60.64
125.00	23.34	31.04	35.74	45.39	35.09	42.79	47.49	57.14
130.00	19.84	27.54	32.24	41.89	31.59	39.29	43.99	53.64
135.00	16.34	24.04	28.74	38.39	28.09	35.79	40.49	50.14
140.00	12.84	20.54	25.24	34.89	24.59	32.29	36.99	46.64
145.00	9.34	17.04	21.74	31.39	21.09	28.79	33.49	43.14
150.00	5.84	13.54	18.24	27.89	17.59	25.29	29.99	39.64
155.00	2.34	10.04	14.74	24.39	14.09	21.79	26.49	36.14
160.00		6.54	11.24	20.89	10.59	18.29	22.99	32.64
165.00		3.04	7.74	17.39	7.09	14.79	19.49	29.14
170.00			4.24	13.89	3.59	11.29	15.99	25.64
175.00			.74	10.39	.09	7.79	12.49	22.14
180.00				6.89		4.29	8.99	18.64
185.00				3.39		.79	5.49	15.14
190.00							1.99	11.64
195.00								8.14
200.00								4.64
205.00								1.14
210.00								
215.00								
220.00								
225.00								
230.00								
235.00								
240.00								
245.00								
250.00								
255.00								
260.00								
265.00								
270.00								
E2	157.63	168.63	175.34	189.13	174.41	185.41	192.13	205.91

Adult Credit £46.45

A - U11 - £11.75
B - 11-15 - £19.45
C - 16-17 - £24.15
D - 18 - £33.80

* These tables are only estimates. They do not take account of the extra premium for people who work 30 hours or more per week

BB	BC	CC	CD	DD	AAA	AAB	AAC	AAD
86.35	90.05	94.75	104.40	114.05	81.70	89.40	94.10	103.75
82.99	86.69	91.39	101.04	110.69	78.34	86.04	90.74	100.39
79.49	83.19	87.89	97.54	107.19	74.84	82.54	87.24	96.89
75.99	79.69	84.39	94.04	103.69	71.34	79.04	83.74	93.39
72.49	76.19	80.89	90.54	100.19	67.84	75.54	80.24	89.89
68.99	72.69	77.39	87.04	96.69	64.34	72.04	76.74	86.39
65.49	69.19	73.89	83.54	93.19	60.84	68.54	73.24	82.89
61.99	65.69	70.39	80.04	89.69	57.34	65.04	69.74	79.39
58.49	62.19	66.89	76.54	86.19	53.84	61.54	66.24	75.89
54.99	58.69	63.39	73.04	82.69	50.34	58.04	62.74	72.39
51.49	55.19	59.89	69.54	79.19	46.84	54.54	59.24	68.89
47.99	51.69	56.39	66.04	75.69	43.34	51.04	55.74	65.39
44.49	48.19	52.89	62.54	72.19	39.84	47.54	52.24	61.89
40.99	44.69	49.39	59.04	68.69	36.34	44.04	48.74	58.39
37.49	41.19	45.89	55.54	65.19	32.84	40.54	45.24	54.89
33.99	37.69	42.39	52.04	61.69	29.34	37.04	41.74	51.39
30.49	34.19	38.89	48.54	58.19	25.84	33.54	38.24	47.89
26.99	30.69	35.39	45.04	54.69	22.34	30.04	34.74	44.39
23.49	27.19	31.89	41.54	51.19	18.84	26.54	31.24	40.89
19.99	23.69	28.39	38.04	47.69	15.34	23.04	27.74	37.39
16.49	20.19	24.89	34.54	44.19	11.84	19.54	24.24	33.89
12.99	16.69	21.39	31.04	40.69	8.34	16.04	20.74	30.39
9.49	13.19	17.89	27.54	37.19	4.84	12.54	17.24	26.89
5.99	9.69	14.39	24.04	33.69	1.34	9.04	13.74	23.39
2.49	6.19	10.89	20.54	30.19		5.54	10.24	19.89
	2.69	7.39	17.04	26.69		2.04	6.74	16.39
		3.89	13.54	23.19			3.24	12.89
		.39	10.04	19.69				9.39
			6.54	16.19				5.89
			3.04	12.69				2.39
				9.19				
				5.69				
				2.19				
197.84	203.13	209.84	223.63	237.41	191.20	202.20	208.91	222.70

Family Credit Ready Reckoner 1996/97

Income	ABB	ABC	ABD	ACC	ACD	ADD	BBB	BBC
75.20	97.10	101.80	111.45	106.50	116.15	125.80	104.80	109.50
80.00	93.74	98.44	108.09	103.14	112.79	122.44	101.44	106.14
85.00	90.24	94.94	104.59	99.64	109.29	118.94	97.94	102.64
90.00	86.74	91.44	101.09	96.14	105.79	115.44	94.44	99.14
95.00	83.24	87.94	97.59	92.64	102.29	111.94	90.94	95.64
100.00	79.74	84.44	94.09	89.14	98.79	108.44	87.44	92.14
105.00	76.24	80.94	90.59	85.64	95.29	104.94	83.94	88.64
110.00	72.74	77.44	87.09	82.14	91.79	101.44	80.44	85.14
115.00	69.24	73.94	83.59	78.64	88.29	97.94	76.94	81.64
120.00	65.74	70.44	80.09	75.14	84.79	94.44	73.44	78.14
125.00	62.24	66.94	78.59	71.64	81.29	90.94	69.94	74.64
130.00	58.74	63.44	73.09	68.14	77.79	87.44	66.44	71.14
135.00	55.24	59.94	69.59	64.64	74.29	83.94	62.94	67.64
140.00	51.74	56.44	66.09	61.14	70.79	80.44	59.44	64.14
145.00	48.24	52.94	62.59	57.64	67.29	76.94	55.94	60.64
150.00	44.74	49.44	59.09	54.14	63.79	73.44	52.44	57.14
155.00	41.24	45.94	55.59	50.64	60.29	69.94	48.94	53.64
160.00	37.74	42.44	52.09	47.14	56.79	66.44	45.44	50.14
165.00	34.24	38.94	48.59	43.64	53.29	62.94	41.94	46.64
170.00	30.74	35.44	45.09	40.14	49.79	59.44	38.44	43.14
175.00	27.24	31.94	41.59	36.64	46.29	55.94	34.94	39.64
180.00	23.74	28.44	38.09	33.14	42.79	52.44	31.44	36.14
185.00	20.24	24.94	34.59	29.64	39.29	48.94	27.94	32.64
190.00	16.74	21.44	31.09	26.14	35.79	45.44	24.44	29.14
195.00	13.24	17.94	27.59	22.64	32.29	41.94	20.94	25.64
200.00	9.74	14.44	24.09	19.14	28.79	38.44	17.44	22.14
205.00	6.24	10.94	20.59	15.64	25.29	34.94	13.94	18.64
210.00	2.74	7.44	17.09	12.14	21.79	31.44	10.44	15.14
215.00		3.94	13.59	8.64	18.29	27.94	6.94	11.64
220.00		.44	10.09	5.14	14.79	24.44	3.44	8.14
225.00			6.59	1.64	11.29	20.94		4.64
230.00			3.09		7.79	17.44		1.14
235.00					4.29	13.94		
240.00					.79	10.44		
245.00						6.94		
250.00						3.44		
255.00								
260.00								
265.00								
270.00								
E2	213.20	219.91	233.70	226.63	240.41	254.20	224.20	230.91

Adult Credit £46.45

A - U11 - £11.75
B - 11-15 - £19.45
C - 16-17 - £24.15
D - 18 - £33.80

* These tables are only estimates. They do not take account of the extra premium for people who work 30 hours or more per week

BBD	BCD	BDD	CCC	CCD	CDD	DDD	AAAA	AAAB
119.15	123.85	133.50	118.90	128.55	138.20	147.85	93.45	101.15
115.79	120.49	130.14	115.54	125.19	134.84	144.49	90.09	97.79
112.29	116.99	126.64	112.04	121.69	131.34	140.99	86.59	94.29
108.79	113.49	123.14	108.54	118.19	127.84	137.49	83.09	90.79
105.29	109.99	119.64	105.04	114.69	124.34	133.99	79.59	87.29
101.79	106.49	116.14	101.54	111.19	120.84	130.49	76.09	83.79
98.29	102.99	112.64	98.04	107.69	117.34	126.99	72.59	80.29
94.79	99.49	109.14	94.54	104.19	113.84	123.49	69.09	76.79
91.29	95.99	105.64	91.04	100.69	110.34	119.99	65.59	73.29
87.79	92.49	102.14	87.54	97.19	106.84	116.49	62.09	69.79
84.29	88.99	98.64	84.04	93.69	103.34	112.99	58.59	66.29
80.79	85.49	95.14	80.54	90.19	99.84	109.49	55.09	62.79
77.29	81.99	91.64	77.04	86.69	96.34	105.99	51.59	59.29
73.79	78.49	88.14	73.54	83.19	92.84	102.49	48.09	55.79
70.29	74.99	84.64	70.04	79.69	89.34	98.99	44.59	52.29
66.79	71.49	81.14	66.54	76.19	85.84	95.49	41.09	48.79
63.29	67.99	77.64	63.04	72.69	82.34	91.99	37.59	45.29
59.79	64.49	74.14	59.54	69.19	78.84	88.49	34.09	41.79
56.29	60.99	70.64	56.04	65.69	75.34	84.99	30.59	38.29
52.79	57.49	67.14	52.54	62.19	71.84	81.49	27.09	34.79
49.29	53.99	63.64	49.04	58.69	68.34	77.99	23.59	31.29
45.79	50.49	60.14	45.54	55.19	64.84	74.49	20.09	27.79
42.29	46.99	56.64	42.04	51.69	61.34	70.99	16.59	24.29
38.79	43.49	53.14	38.54	48.19	57.84	67.49	13.09	20.79
35.29	39.99	49.64	35.04	44.69	54.34	63.99	9.59	17.29
31.79	36.49	46.14	31.54	41.19	50.84	60.49	6.09	13.79
28.29	32.99	42.64	28.04	37.69	47.34	56.99	2.59	10.29
24.79	29.49	39.14	24.54	34.19	43.84	53.49		6.79
21.29	25.99	35.64	21.04	30.69	40.34	49.99		3.29
17.79	22.49	32.14	17.54	27.19	36.84	46.49		
14.29	18.99	28.64	14.04	23.69	33.34	42.99		
10.79	15.49	25.14	10.54	20.19	29.84	39.49		
7.29	11.99	21.64	7.04	16.69	26.34	35.99		
3.79	8.49	18.14	3.54	13.19	22.84	32.49		
.29	4.99	14.64	.04	9.69	19.34	28.99		
	1.49	11.14		6.19	15.84	25.49		
		7.64		2.69	12.34	21.99		
		4.14			8.84	18.49		
		.64			5.34	14.99		
					1.84	11.49		
244.70	251.41	265.20	244.34	258.13	271.91	285.70	207.99	218.99

Family Credit Ready Reckoner 1996/97

Income	AAAC	AAAD	AABB	AABC	AABD	AACC	AACD
75.20	105.85	115.50	108.85	113.55	123.20	118.25	127.90
80.00	102.49	112.14	105.49	110.19	119.84	114.89	124.54
85.00	98.99	108.64	101.99	106.69	116.34	111.39	121.04
90.00	95.49	105.14	98.49	103.19	112.84	107.89	117.54
95.00	91.99	101.64	94.99	99.69	109.34	104.39	114.04
100.00	88.49	98.14	91.49	96.19	105.84	100.89	110.54
105.00	84.99	94.64	87.99	92.69	102.34	97.39	107.04
110.00	81.49	91.14	84.49	89.19	98.84	93.89	103.54
115.00	77.99	87.64	80.99	85.69	95.34	90.39	100.04
120.00	74.49	84.14	77.49	82.19	91.84	86.89	96.54
125.00	70.99	80.64	73.99	78.69	88.34	83.39	93.04
130.00	67.49	77.14	70.49	75.19	84.84	79.89	89.54
135.00	63.99	73.64	66.99	71.69	81.34	76.39	86.04
140.00	60.49	70.14	63.49	68.19	77.84	72.89	82.54
145.00	56.99	66.64	59.99	64.69	74.34	69.39	79.04
150.00	53.49	63.14	56.49	61.19	70.84	65.89	75.54
155.00	49.99	59.64	52.99	57.69	67.34	62.39	72.04
160.00	46.49	56.14	49.49	54.19	63.84	58.89	68.54
165.00	42.99	52.64	45.99	50.69	60.34	55.39	65.04
170.00	39.49	49.14	42.49	47.19	56.84	51.89	61.54
175.00	35.99	45.64	38.99	43.69	53.34	48.39	58.04
180.00	32.49	42.14	35.49	40.19	49.84	44.89	54.54
185.00	28.99	38.64	31.99	36.69	46.34	41.39	51.04
190.00	25.49	35.14	28.49	33.19	42.84	37.69	47.54
195.00	21.99	31.64	24.99	29.69	39.34	34.39	44.04
200.00	18.49	28.14	21.49	26.19	35.84	30.89	40.54
205.00	14.99	24.64	17.99	22.69	32.34	27.39	37.04
210.00	11.49	21.14	14.49	19.19	28.84	23.89	33.54
215.00	7.99	17.64	10.99	15.69	25.34	20.39	30.04
220.00	4.49	14.14	7.49	12.19	21.84	16.89	26.54
225.00	.99	10.64	3.99	8.69	18.34	13.39	23.04
230.00		7.14	.49	5.19	14.84	9.89	19.54
235.00		3.64		1.69	11.34	6.39	16.04
240.00		.14			7.84	2.89	12.54
245.00					4.34		9.04
250.00					.84		5.54
255.00							2.04
260.00							
265.00							
270.00							
E2	225.70	239.49	229.99	236.70	250.49	204.84	218.63

Adult Credit £46.45

A - U11 - £11.75
B - 11-15 - £19.45
C - 16-17 - £24.15
D - 18 - £33.80

* These tables are only estimates. They do not take account of the extra premium for people who work 30 hours or more per week

AADD	ABBB	ABBC	ABBD	ABCC	ABCD	ABDD	ACCC
137.55	116.55	121.25	130.90	125.95	135.60	145.25	130.65
134.19	113.19	117.89	127.54	122.59	132.24	141.89	127.29
130.69	109.69	114.39	124.04	119.09	128.74	138.39	123.79
127.19	106.19	110.89	120.54	115.59	125.24	134.89	120.29
123.69	102.69	107.39	117.04	112.09	121.74	131.39	116.79
120.19	99.19	103.89	113.54	108.59	118.24	127.89	113.29
116.69	95.69	100.39	110.04	105.09	114.74	124.39	109.79
113.19	92.19	96.89	106.54	101.59	111.24	120.89	106.29
109.69	88.69	93.39	103.04	98.09	107.74	117.39	102.79
106.19	85.19	89.89	99.54	94.59	104.24	113.89	99.29
102.69	81.69	86.39	96.04	91.09	100.74	110.39	95.79
99.19	78.19	82.89	92.54	87.59	97.24	106.89	92.29
95.69	74.69	79.39	89.04	84.09	93.74	103.39	88.79
92.19	71.19	75.89	85.54	80.59	90.24	99.89	85.29
88.69	67.69	72.39	82.04	77.09	86.74	96.39	81.79
85.19	64.19	68.89	78.54	73.59	83.24	92.89	78.29
81.69	60.69	65.39	75.04	70.09	79.74	89.39	74.79
78.19	57.19	61.89	71.54	66.59	76.24	85.89	71.29
74.69	53.69	58.39	68.04	63.09	72.74	82.39	67.79
71.19	50.19	54.89	64.54	59.59	69.24	78.89	64.29
67.69	46.69	51.39	61.04	56.59	65.74	75.39	60.79
64.19	43.19	47.89	57.54	52.59	62.24	71.89	57.29
60.69	39.69	44.39	54.04	49.09	58.74	68.39	53.79
57.19	36.19	40.89	50.54	45.59	55.24	64.89	50.29
53.69	32.69	37.39	47.04	42.09	51.74	61.39	46.79
50.19	29.19	33.89	43.54	38.59	48.24	57.89	43.29
46.69	25.69	30.39	40.04	35.09	44.74	54.39	39.79
43.19	22.19	26.89	36.54	31.59	41.24	50.89	36.29
39.69	18.69	23.39	33.04	28.09	37.74	47.39	32.79
36.19	15.19	19.89	29.54	24.59	34.24	43.89	29.29
32.69	11.69	16.39	26.04	21.09	30.74	40.39	25.79
29.19	8.19	12.89	22.54	17.59	27.24	36.89	22.29
25.69	4.69	9.39	19.04	14.09	23.74	33.39	18.79
22.19	1.19	5.89	15.54	10.59	20.24	29.89	15.29
18.69		2.39	12.04	7.09	16.74	26.39	11.79
15.19			8.54	3.59	13.24	22.89	8.29
11.69			5.04	.09	9.74	19.39	4.79
8.19			1.54		6.24	15.89	1.29
4.69					2.74	12.39	
1.19						8.89	
232.41	202.41	209.13	222.91	215.84	229.63	243.41	222.56

Family Credit Ready Reckoner 1996/97

Income	ACCD	ACDD	ADDD	BBBB	BBBC	BBBD	BBCC
75.20	140.30	149.95	159.60	124.25	128.95	138.60	133.65
80.00	136.94	146.59	156.24	120.89	125.59	135.24	130.29
85.00	133.44	143.09	152.74	117.39	122.09	131.74	126.79
90.00	129.94	139.59	149.24	113.89	118.59	128.24	123.29
95.00	126.44	136.09	145.74	110.39	115.09	124.74	119.79
100.00	122.94	132.59	142.24	106.89	111.59	121.24	116.29
105.00	119.44	129.09	138.74	103.39	108.09	117.74	112.79
110.00	115.94	125.59	135.24	99.89	104.59	114.24	109.29
115.00	112.44	122.09	131.74	96.39	101.09	110.74	105.79
120.00	108.94	118.59	128.24	92.89	97.59	107.24	102.29
125.00	105.44	115.09	124.74	89.39	94.09	103.74	98.79
130.00	101.94	111.59	121.24	85.89	90.59	100.24	95.29
135.00	98.44	108.09	117.74	82.39	87.09	96.74	91.79
140.00	94.94	104.59	114.24	78.89	83.59	93.24	88.29
145.00	91.44	101.09	110.74	75.39	80.09	89.74	84.79
150.00	87.94	97.59	107.24	71.89	76.59	86.24	81.29
155.00	84.44	94.09	103.74	68.39	73.09	82.74	77.79
160.00	80.94	90.59	100.24	64.89	69.59	79.24	74.29
165.00	77.44	87.09	96.74	61.39	66.09	75.74	70.79
170.00	73.94	83.59	93.24	57.89	62.59	72.24	67.29
175.00	70.44	80.09	89.74	54.39	59.09	68.74	63.79
180.00	66.94	76.59	86.24	50.89	55.59	65.24	60.29
185.00	63.44	73.09	82.74	47.39	52.09	61.74	56.79
190.00	59.94	69.59	79.24	43.89	48.59	58.24	53.29
195.00	56.44	66.09	75.74	40.39	45.09	54.74	49.79
200.00	52.94	62.59	72.24	36.89	41.59	51.24	46.29
205.00	49.44	59.09	68.74	33.39	38.09	47.74	42.79
210.00	45.94	55.59	65.24	29.89	34.59	44.24	39.29
215.00	42.44	52.09	61.74	26.39	31.09	40.74	35.79
220.00	38.94	48.59	58.24	22.89	27.59	37.24	32.29
225.00	35.44	45.09	54.74	19.39	24.09	33.74	28.79
230.00	31.94	41.59	51.24	15.89	20.59	30.24	25.29
235.00	28.44	38.09	47.74	12.39	17.09	26.74	21.79
240.00	24.94	34.59	44.24	8.89	13.59	23.24	18.29
245.00	21.44	31.09	40.74	5.39	10.09	19.74	14.79
250.00	17.94	27.59	37.24	1.89	6.59	16.24	11.29
255.00	14.44	24.09	33.74		3.09	12.74	7.79
260.00	10.94	20.59	30.24			9.24	4.29
265.00	7.44	17.09	26.74			5.74	.79
270.00	3.94	13.59	23.24			2.24	
E2	236.34	250.13	263.91	213.41	220.13	233.91	226.84

Adult Credit £46.45

A - U11 - £11.75
B - 11-15 - £19.45
C - 16-17 - £24.15
D - 18 - £33.80

* These tables are only estimates. They do not take account of the extra premium for people who work 30 hours or more per week

BBCD	BBDD	BCCC	BCCD	BCDD	BDDD	CCCC	CCCD
143.30	152.95	138.35	148.00	157.65	167.30	143.05	152.70
139.94	149.59	134.99	144.64	154.29	163.94	139.69	149.34
136.44	146.09	131.49	141.14	150.79	160.44	136.19	145.84
132.94	142.59	127.99	137.64	147.29	156.94	132.69	142.34
129.44	139.09	124.49	134.14	143.79	153.44	129.19	138.84
125.94	135.59	120.99	130.64	140.29	149.94	125.69	135.34
122.44	132.09	117.49	127.14	136.79	146.44	122.19	131.84
118.94	128.59	113.99	123.64	133.29	142.94	118.69	128.34
115.44	125.09	110.49	120.14	129.79	139.44	115.19	124.84
111.94	121.59	106.99	116.64	126.29	135.94	111.69	121.34
108.44	118.09	103.49	113.14	122.79	132.44	108.19	117.84
104.94	114.59	99.99	109.64	119.29	128.94	104.69	114.34
101.44	111.09	96.49	106.14	115.79	125.44	101.19	110.84
97.94	107.59	92.99	102.64	112.29	121.94	97.69	107.34
94.44	104.09	89.49	99.14	108.79	118.44	94.19	103.84
90.94	100.59	85.99	95.64	105.29	114.94	90.69	100.34
87.44	97.09	82.49	92.14	101.79	111.44	87.19	96.84
83.94	93.59	78.99	88.64	98.29	107.94	83.69	93.34
80.44	90.09	75.49	85.14	94.79	104.44	80.19	89.84
76.94	86.59	71.99	81.64	91.29	100.94	76.69	86.34
73.44	83.09	68.49	78.14	87.79	97.44	73.19	82.84
69.94	79.59	64.99	74.64	84.29	93.94	69.69	79.34
66.44	76.09	61.49	71.14	80.79	90.44	66.19	75.84
62.94	72.59	57.99	67.64	77.29	86.94	62.69	72.34
59.44	69.09	54.49	64.14	73.79	83.44	59.19	68.84
55.94	65.59	50.99	60.64	70.29	79.94	55.69	65.34
52.44	62.09	47.49	57.14	66.79	76.44	52.19	61.84
48.94	58.59	43.99	53.64	63.29	72.94	48.69	58.34
45.44	55.09	40.49	50.14	59.79	69.44	45.19	54.84
41.94	51.59	36.99	46.64	56.29	65.94	41.69	51.34
38.44	48.09	33.49	43.14	52.79	62.44	38.19	47.84
34.94	44.59	29.99	39.64	49.29	58.94	34.69	44.34
31.44	41.09	26.49	36.14	45.79	55.44	31.19	40.84
27.94	37.59	22.99	32.64	42.29	51.94	27.69	37.34
24.44	34.09	19.49	29.14	38.79	48.44	24.19	33.84
20.94	30.59	15.99	25.64	35.29	44.94	20.69	30.34
17.44	27.09	12.49	22.14	31.79	41.44	17.19	26.84
13.94	23.59	8.99	18.64	28.29	37.94	13.69	23.34
10.44	20.09	5.49	15.14	24.79	34.44	10.19	19.84
6.94	16.59	1.99	11.64	21.29	30.94	6.69	16.34
240.63	254.41	272.13	285.91	299.70	313.49	278.84	292.63

Family Credit Ready Reckoner 1996/97

Income	CCDD	CDDD	DDDD
75.20	162.35	172.00	181.65
80.00	158.99	168.64	178.29
85.00	155.49	165.14	174.79
90.00	151.99	161.64	171.29
95.00	148.49	158.14	167.79
100.00	144.99	154.64	164.29
105.00	141.49	151.14	160.79
110.00	137.99	147.64	157.29
115.00	134.49	144.14	153.79
120.00	130.99	140.64	150.29
125.00	127.49	137.14	146.79
130.00	123.99	133.64	143.29
135.00	120.49	130.14	139.79
140.00	116.99	126.64	136.29
145.00	113.49	123.14	132.79
150.00	109.99	119.64	129.29
155.00	106.49	116.14	125.79
160.00	102.99	112.64	122.29
165.00	99.49	109.14	118.79
170.00	95.99	105.64	115.29
175.00	92.49	102.14	111.79
180.00	88.99	98.64	108.29
185.00	85.49	95.14	104.79
190.00	81.99	91.64	101.29
195.00	78.49	88.14	97.79
200.00	74.99	84.64	94.29
205.00	71.49	81.14	90.79
210.00	67.99	77.64	87.29
215.00	64.49	74.14	83.79
220.00	60.99	70.64	80.29
225.00	57.49	67.14	76.79
230.00	53.99	63.64	73.29
235.00	50.49	60.14	69.79
240.00	46.99	56.64	66.29
245.00	43.49	53.14	62.79
250.00	39.99	49.64	59.29
255.00	36.49	46.14	55.79
260.00	32.99	42.64	52.29
265.00	29.49	39.14	48.79
270.00	25.99	35.64	45.29
E2	306.41	320.20	333.99

Adult Credit £46.45

A - U11 - £11.75
B - 11-15 - £19.45
C - 16-17 - £24.15
D - 18 - £33.80

* These tables are only estimates. They do not take account of the extra premium for people who work 30 hours or more per week

Section 3 Contents

Page

Unemployed and seeking work

Section
3

Employment

Introduction

Leaflet 'Just the Job', available from local Job Centres

Restart Programme

Counselling interviews and courses to help long-term unemployed.

Open to

People aged 18 and over who have been unemployed for 6 months or more.

Contact

The local Job Centre will make contact with the customer.

Job Clubs

Coaching in job hunting techniques, support and motivation for people to look for work. Job Clubs have the use of desk, telephone, typewriter, directories, stationery, postage etc, free of charge. Special language and literacy groups now exist for those with special needs. Specialist Job Clubs, eg for professional and executive groups, homeless or deaf people, exist in some areas.

Open to

People aged 18 and over with no upper age limit. Normally they must have been unemployed for at least 6 months but special rules apply to ex-regulars, people with disabilities, literacy or numeracy difficulties, ex-offenders, returners to the labour market and those needing help with basic English.

Contact

The local Job Centre.

Travel to Interview Scheme

Financial help for those who need to travel to job interviews beyond their normal area.

Open to

People who have been unemployed for more than 4 weeks and are applying for a full time job expected to last a year or more.

Contact

The local Job Centre.

Community Action

Community Action acts as a stepping stone back into work. It is a voluntary programme which provides placements in projects dealing with environmental and conservation initiatives.

Open to

People who have been unemployed for 12 months or more.

Contact

The local Job Centre.

Work Trials

This provides an opportunity to take up employment with an employer who has a vacancy to fill. The trial usually lasts up to six weeks during which time the employee can see if they like the job and the employer feels that they are suited to it. Benefit continues in payment plus travel costs of up to £10 a day and meal expenses.

Open to

People who have been unemployed for more than 6 months. Other people such as those who have a disability, or are an ex-offender can apply earlier.

Contact

The local Job Centre.

Jobfinders Grant

A payment of £200 (except in the South West and Yorks & Humberside). Can be affected by capital. Is repayable if work ceases within 8 weeks.

Open to

People who have been unemployed and in receipt of either UB, IS, SDA, IB, NI Credits for at least 2 years and :-

- have earnings of less than £150 per week gross

- work 30 hours or more per week

- expect to be in work for 6 months or more

- Are not self employed

Contact

The local Job Centre.

Enterprise

Enterprise grant scheme/'self start'

Financial help to support unemployed people who want to become self-employed or start their own small business. Grants can vary from area to area.

It could average between £20 - £90 a week. Further information can be obtained from Training Enterprise Council (TEC).

Tourism

Help and advice with tourism projects open to those seeking a career or business opportunity in tourism.

Contact

Tourism Board or Training Commission Area office.

Loan Guarantee Scheme

Government guarantees for bank loans made to businesses.

Open to

Owner managers of most small businesses.

Contact

Bank managers.

Career Development Loans

Career development loans are available to help people who want to take responsibility for meeting their own training needs, to pay for a course themselves. Help is available for up to 80% of the course fees plus full costs of books and materials and living expenses where appropriate.

Loans are available from £200 - £8000 through selected banks.

Open to

Anyone over 18 who lives or intends to train in Great Britain.

Contact

Local Job Centre.

Ring for a booklet 0800 585 505.

Training Enterprise Council (TEC) will give more information.

Training

Youth Training

YT provides training and planned work experience for school leavers (16 and 17 year olds) in almost any type of job. Training is given by specialist training firms, employers, colleges of further education, Local Authorities and voluntary basis.

It also provides the opportunity to gain a qualification (NVQ).

Persons 18 or over who have not been able to take up a place earlier because of disability, ill health, pregnancy, custodial sentence, language difficulty or care order are also guaranteed an offer on YT. Even if 18 year olds do not come into this category they can still apply for a place. They should check with Job Centres for details.

16 and 17 year olds receive a tax free allowance of £29.50 per week if aged 16 and £35.00 for 17 or over.

In England Youth Credits can be given to young people to buy their own training. They should check with their Job Centre to see if credits are available in the area.

Contact

Local Careers Office/TEC

Training for Work

This provides an opportunity to gain work experience that is directly related to the work somone wants to do.

Usually someone would enrol as part of their Restart Interview, where a training programme is designed for that person's needs. Often the training will work towards the person gaining an NVQ or being in temporary work.

An allowance equivalent to any benefit being paid will be made plus an additional £10 a week and sometimes help towards travel costs and childcare.

Open to

All adults between 18 and 63 years of age who have been unemployed for 6 months or more.

Earlier entry for:

- unemployed people with disabilities

- people returning to the labour market

- ex- service personnel recently leaving HM forces

- people receiving training in English as a second language

- single people on Social Security order books with school age children

- people seeking training in high-tech skills or enterprise

Contact

The local Job Centre.

Small Business Development Scheme

Provides training for the owner/manager for existing small businesses.

Open to

Suitable employed or self-employed people over 18 (graduates regardless of employment status in the case of the Graduate Enterprise Programme).

For people interested in starting their own business, Employment Training also offers enterprise training.

Contact

Training Commission Area Office.

Business Enterprise Program

Free start-up for small business.

Open to

Employed and unemployed. If unemployed, BEP may be found within ET without the requirement to be unemployed for 6 months.

Contact

TEC

Training Grants for Employers

A wide range of practical and financial help for training employees and new recruits.

Open to

Employers with priority for some cases for small firms

Contact

TEC

Open Learning

Allows people to learn at their own pace, either at home or at work.

Open to

Employed and unemployed and employers who want to use OpenLearning to train employees (see Training Grants for employers)

Contact

Local Job Centre, public library or TEC

Note

There are 82 Training & Enterprise Councils (TEC) in England & Wales (or Local Enterprise Companies(LEC) in Scotland). They provide business and enterprise services and training or re-training to people of all ages.

Training Access Points (TAPs) can be found in local libraries and Jobcentres which provide a database giving details of training and education opportunities in the area.

Redundancy Payments

Introduction

D of E Booklet 16 (Employers)

D of E leaflet PL 73 (Employees)

A lump sum payment paid by the employer which is not normally taxed as it falls below the tax threshold for such payments (currently £30,000).

Redundancy Payments do not attract National Insurance contributions. Employers do not receive any reimbursement.

Conditions

* must be continuously employed for 2 years since reaching age 18

* the employee must be redundant and has not refused suitable alternative employment

* if not paid automatically claims must be made in writing within 6 months

* payments are reduced if the employee is within 12 months of retirement age

* women of 60 years or over may claim a redundancy payment

Payment rate

This depends on the number of years employment, the employee's age and his rate of pay.

For each year of employment when the employee was aged at least 41 - 64 he receives 1½ x weeks pay (to a maximum of £210 per week).

Between 22 + 40 he receives 1 x weeks pay (to a maximum of £210 per week).

Age 18 - 21 he receives ½ x weeks pay (to a maximum of £210 per week).

Unemployed and seeking work

A maximum of 20 years service can be counted.

Redundancy enquiries: 0800 848 489

Unemployment Benefit

Introduction

Leaflet NI 12

Contributory taxable

Customer must be unemployed, signing-on and ready, willing and able, ie available to take up full-time work. A customer must also show that he is actively seeking work.

Based on contributions in the two relevant tax years which are the last two complete tax years before the benefit year in which a Period of Interruption of Employment starts (PIE).

The benefit year starts the first Sunday in January.

Note: Unemployment Benefit (UB) will be replaced by Jobseeker's Allowance from October 1996.

Contributions conditions

(1)   Must have paid Class 1 contributions on earnings on at least 25 times the weekly lower earnings limit in at least one of the two relevant years (credits do not count for this condition); and

(2)   must have paid or been credited with Class 1 contributions on earnings of at least 50 times the weekly lower earnings limit in each of the 2 relevant tax years (credits do count for this condition).

Period payable

Unemployment Benefit is payable for a maximum of 312 days (52 x 6 day weeks) in any one 'period of interruption of employment'. For new claims from 8th April 1996, UB will be a 7 day benefit and payable for a maximum of 26 weeks (182 days).

Unemployed and seeking work

Section
3

Payment of benefit will not resume until the customer has worked at least 13 weeks for 16 hours or more (need not be continuous). The 13 weeks work must normally all fall within the 26 complete weeks (Sunday to Saturday) immediately before the week of the day of claim of the first effective day of unemployment.

Rate

Customer	£48.25
Adult dependant	£29.75 (As long as dependant is not earning more than this amount)
Child	Nil
Customer over pension age	£61.15
Adult dependant	£36.60 (As long as dependant is not earning more than this amount)
Eldest child	£9.90
Each subsequent child	£11.15

Disqualification

Benefit may not be paid for the first 26 weeks after leaving a job voluntarily without good reason or following dismissal for misconduct. Under the 'Employment on Trial' provision a job may be taken without risk of loss of benefit provided the customer was not sacked through misconduct or similar situations.

On a new claim, a customer will be allowed to restrict his job search to his usual occupation and rate of pay for up to 13 weeks.

After this 'permitted period' the customer would be expected to broaden the range of jobs sought. Refusal of a job offered by an Employment Service Counsellor may result in disqualification of UB for up to 26 weeks, if good cause is not established.

Pay in lieu of notice and certain other income may also delay the award of benefit. A claim should always be registered, nevertheless.

Other income

Where earnings equal or exceed the LEL (£61) in any benefit week, UB will not be paid. Also where earnings are in excess of £2 a day, this will result in the loss of that day's UB (including Sundays from April 1996).

If the customer is 55 or over then an occupational pension of over £35 per week gross will reduce the rate of benefit.

Credits

Credits are usually awarded for each complete week (Monday to Saturday) when someone is:

- unemployed
- capable of work
- available for employment
- actively seeking employment

If UB is in payment credits are awarded automatically.

Confirmation should be sought from the ESJ regarding entitlement to credits.

Where there is a disallowance under SS Acts (ie during periods where the customer voluntarily left work) or where a reduced rate election is in force, no credits of any description are awarded. However credits are awarded now despite redundancy payments, even when benefit is disallowed due to wages in lieu.

Other benefits

UB will affect entitlement to other NI benefits. Income Support can be paid during the periods of disqualification for leaving work without good cause, but at a reduced rate.

Unemployed and seeking work

Students

Full-time students are not entitled to register as unemployed during vacations (except the summer vacation following the final term of the course).

Student couples with children may be able to receive Income Support (if signing as unemployed) during summer vacations.

Jobseeker's Allowance

Background

Under the new Act, Jobseeker's Allowance (JSA) will replace Unemployment Benefit and Income Support for unemployed people from October 1996.

Under JSA customers who qualify for benefit because they satisfy the National Insurance Contribution conditions will receive a personal allowance for a maximum of six months.

Those who do not satisfy the contribution conditions at the start of a claim or those whose 6 month period of contribution based JSA has exhausted or those who are entitled to contribution based JSA but have requirements greater than that amount may be eligible for income based JSA.

A period of 3 "waiting days" is applied before payment starts for both contribution based (CB) and income based (IB) JSA.

Looking for work

The jobseeker will be expected to agree to a "jobseeker's agreement" based on the jobsearch plan which will be discussed at the "new jobseeker" interview.

Normally the jobseeker will attend fortnightly thereafter for a jobsearch review. If the conditions for JSA are still being met, benefit will be paid.

If it appears that the jobseeker is "voluntarily" unemployed (ie lost job through misconduct or refuses a job without good cause) a **sanction** can be imposed which stops payment of JSA for up to 26 weeks. Payment at a reduced can be made if hardship would arise, but this must be claimed for.

Employment on trial

People who were previously unemployed for more than 13 weeks may leave a job where they were employed for over 4 weeks but less than 12 without a sanction being imposed.

Requalification

Rules that allowed requalification of UB will not apply to JSA.

Short-term sickness

JSA can be paid for up to two periods of 2 weeks sickness within a 12 month period.

Earnings rules

The rules that apply to IS are the same for JSA.

The CB part of JSA will not be affected by a partner's earnings. If the jobseeker's partner works less than 24 hours a week, IB JSA can still be paid (subject to the partner's earnings etc).

Students

Jobseekers can receive JSA if studying part-time and are actively seeking work. For FEFC funded courses, part-time is defined as 16 hours or less per week of guided learning.

Occupational pensions

With CB JSA, all occupational and personal pensions above the threshold of £50 a week could affect the amount payable, regardless of the age of the jobseeker.

For IB JSA, occupational and personal pensions are taken fully into account.

Credits

Under JSA, jobseekers who work less than 16 hours a week will get NI credits.

JSA abroad

The CB part of JSA is exportable for up to 3 months subject to EC law.

IB JSA is not.

Deductions

Deductions for social fund repayments, overpayments etc can be made from CB and IB JSA. Deductions for housing costs, fuel etc can normally only be made from IB JSA.

Transitional arrangements/protection

For a jobseeker to get transitional protection, UB and/or IS must be payable for the 5th or 6th October 1996. In addition, if UB is payable on 7/4/96 the balance of 312 days benefit may be paid. However, if a new claim to UB is made on or after 8/4/96 a maximum of 182 days benefit can be paid.

The cut-off date for transitional protection will be w/c 7/4/97. Therefore once a jobseeker has established entitlement to transitional protection, they can regain entitlement if a new claim links with a previous one.

Back to Work Bonus

This scheme will be introduced in October 1996.

The Back to Work Bonus will enable people who are working part-time to build up a lump sum equivelant to half their part-time earnings (after disregards), payable when they start work and cease benefit.

The maximum amount payable will be £1000.

The customer must have been in receipt of Income Support or JSA for 91 days or more.

Section 4 Contents

Page

Income Support and Social Fund

Section
4

Income Support

Introduction

Leaflets IS1& IS20

Claim forms A1/B1/SP1

Income related benefit

Income Support (IS) is a Social Security benefit to help people who do not have enough money to live on.

Main Income Support rules

Most people have to satisfy the following rules to get Income Support:

*   aged 18 years, or over

*   16 and 17 year old may be eligible in certain circumstances

*   resident in Great Britain

*   habitual residence test

*   not engaged in remunerative work*+

*   partner not engaged in remunerative work*

*   no more than £8,000 savings (£16000 if in a residential/nursing home)

* Unless the customer or their partner works as a daytime childminder in their own home.

+ Remunerative work has been redefined as 16 hours per week from April 1992. (However, there is indefinite protection for people who were already working over 16 hours but under 24 hours).

Who can get Income Support?

The main groups of people who Income Support is designed to help include:

* people aged 60 years or over

* people who are unemployed and available for work

* people who cannot work because of sickness or disability

* lone parents

* people who have to look after someone who is elderly, sick, or disabled

Couples - either can claim if they meet the conditions of entitlement.

Note

From October 1996, JSA will replace Income Support for those "signing-on" as unemployed and for partners renumerative work will be 24 hours a week or more.

16 and 17 year Olds

Leaflet IS26

Most 16-17 year olds are not able to get Income Support. Instead, they are guaranteed a place on Youth Training.

Special groups of young people can get Income Support if:

* they are expecting a baby in 11 weeks or less

* they are a lone parent looking after his/her child

* they are incapable of work or training due to illness or disability

* they are registered blind

* they are estranged from their parents

* they have no living parents and no-one acting as a parent

* they have recently been in care or placed away from home by the probation service

- they are a refugee learning English who has been in the UK for less than a year

- in non-advanced education and are severely handicapped, orphaned or estranged

- carers

- temporarily laid off employment

- they are not in the above groups but would otherwise suffer unavoidable severe hardship

Making a claim

People who do not have to sign on for work can make their initial claim for Income Support in several ways:

- by tear-off coupon attached to leaflet IS1 available from post office and local   Benefits Agency offices

- by letter to the local Benefits Agency office

- by calling in at the local Benefits Agency office

- by phoning Freeline on 0800 666 555

A claim form can also be obtained by telephoning the office. This must be returned within one month.

People who register for work and want to claim Income Support should ask their Employment Services Jobcentre (ESJ) for form B1 which is completed and returned to the local Benefits Agency office within one month.

Decisions

Decisions on claims are decided by Adjudication Officers. Customers are asked to provide information to assess the claim including proof of:

- earnings

- savings

- expenses

- occupational pensions

- if a person is a owner occupier, verification of the mortgage is needed

- identity

Customers receive a summary of how their benefit has been worked out. A more detailed explanation can be obtained from the Benefits Agency office making the payment.

Appeals

Customers have the right of appeal to an independent Social Security Appeal Tribunal. Appeals should be made in writing to a Benefits Agency office within 3 months of the decision, giving the reasons for the appeal. Leaflet NI 246 gives more detailed information.

Payment

Every customer is allocated a regular payday for their Income Support payment. Generally if a customer is already getting another benefit, their Income Support is paid to them on the same day as that benefit, ie:

- Retirement Pension

- Widows Benefit

- Incapacity Benefit

- Unemployment Benefit

Most people are paid their Income Support weekly or fortnightly in arrears. Customers are paid weekly in advance if they are getting:

- Retirement Pension; or

- Widows Benefit (unless they are signing on as available for work, or cannot work because of sickness or disability)

- over state pension age (60 for women, 65 for men) and not getting Unemployment Benefit, Incapacity Benefit or Severe Disablement Allowance

Method of payment

There are three main methods of payment

- girocheque

- order book

- automatic credit transfer (ACT) to a bank or building society account

Sick/unemployed customers normally receive their benefit fortnightly in arrears by girocheque or ACT.

Sick/unemployed, disabled lone parents and carers normally receive their benefit weekly in arrears by girocheque, order book or ACT.

People of pension age or those in receipt of Retirement Pension or Widows Pension are normally paid weekly in advance by girocheque, order book or ACT.

Order books are issued automatically to the post office for collection by the customer. Orders have to be cashed within 3 months of the date on them.

Girocheques have to be cashed within one month of the date issued.

Calculation

Payments are made up of all or some of the following parts:

Personal Allowance

A payment to cover the needs of the customer and their partner if they have one and are based on age.

Dependant Allowance for a child or young person

A payment for each child or young person the customer is responsible for, based on age.

Premium Payments

Extra payments for groups of people whose expenses are likely to be higher than normal.

Housing costs

Payments to cover certain costs of accommodation that are not met by Housing Benefit. For owner-occupiers, the weekly equivalent of the 'standard' interest on the loan is paid.

The total of these allowances is known as the applicable amount. Whether this is paid in full depends on other factors such as income or capital.

Allowances

There are different allowances for the people described above. Customers get all the allowances they qualify for.

Single People

• 16 and 17 years old	£28.85
• 16 and 17 years old with good reason for living away from home	£37.90
• 16 and 17 years old entitled to disability premium	£37.90
• 18 to 24 years old	£37.90
• 18 years old and over and bringing up a child on their own	£47.90
• 25 years and over	£47.90

Couples

• both under 18	£57.20
• both of the couple 18 or over (Special rules apply if one or both of the couple is under 18)	£75.20

For each child in the family

• under 11	£16.45
• 11 - 15 years old	£24.10

- 16 - 17 years old on a full-time course not above
  A level/OND standard £28.85

- 18 years old on a full-time course not above
  A level/OND standard £37.90

Premiums

Special additions to the Personal Allowances to help with the extra needs of certain groups.

Family premium, disabled child premium, carer premium and severe disability premium can be paid in addition to any other premium.

The premiums are:

- Family Premium

- Disabled Child Premium

- Carer Premium

- Lone Parent Premium

- Disability Premium

- Pensioner Premium

- Enhanced Pensioner Premium

- Higher Pensioner Premium

- Severe Disability Premium

People with Children

Family Premium

Paid if the customer has at least one dependant child £10.55

Lone Parent Premium

Paid if the customer is bringing up one or more
dependant children on their own £5.20

Disabled Child Premium

Paid for each dependant child receiving DLA or registered blind,

and the child has less than £3,000 savings   £20.40

Long term sick or disabled people

Disability Premium

Paid if the customer or partner:

- receive Incapacity Benefit (long term rate), Severe Disablement Allowance, Disability Living Allowance, Disability Working Allowance or

- are registered blind, or

- if the customer has submitted medical certificates for 365 days, or

- is sick for 28 weeks and terminally ill

    Single   £20.40   Couple   £29.15

Severe Disability Premium

Payable at two rates:

    Single   £36.40   Couple   £72.80

The lower rate is payable to a single customer and lone parents if:

(1)   they receive Attendance Allowance or the middle or higher care component of Disability Living Allowance; and

(2)   they live alone; and

(3)   no one receives Invalid Care Allowance for looking after them.

The higher rate is payable to couples if:

(1)   both partners receive Attendance Allowance or the middle or higher care component of Disability Living Allowance; and

(2)   no one else lives in the household; and

(3)   no one receives Invalid care Allowance for looking after either partner.

If Invalid Care Allowance is paid in respect of only one partner and the other conditions are satisfied, the lower rate Severe Disability Premium is payable.

The lower rate Severe Disability Premium is also payable to couples where one partner receives Attendance Allowance or Disability Living Allowance care component at the middle rate or higher rate and:

(1)   the other partner is blind; and

(2)   Invalid Care Allowance is not payable in respect of caring for the customer.

Certain people living in the household can be ignored for purposes of Severe Disability Premium.

Severe Disability Premium can be paid in addition to Higher Pensioner Premium or Disability Premium.

Carer Premium

Paid if the customer or partner is in receipt of Invalid Care Allowance or would have been if a higher overlapping benefit was not already in payment. £13.00

If both customer and partner are in receipt of Invalid Care Allowance separately, the Carer premium is paid twice.

People aged 60 or over

Pensioner Premium

Paid if the customer or their partner is aged 60 to 74 inclusive.

Single   £19.15   Couple   £28.90

Enhanced Pensioner Premium

Paid if the customer or their partner is aged 75 to 79 inclusive.

Single   £21.30   Couple   £31.90

Higher Pensioner Premium

Paid if the customer or their partner:

(1)   is aged 80 or over; or

(2)   aged 60 or over and one is receiving Disability Living Allowance or Incapacity Benefit (long term rate) or Severe Disablement Allowance or Attendance Allowance or Disability Working Allowance

(3)   satisfied the conditions for receiving the disability premium within 8 weeks of becoming aged 60; or

(4)   registered blind; or

(5)   provided with an invalid carriage.

Single   £25.90   Couple   £37.05

Housing costs

People getting Income Support and who are responsible for housing costs may get help in two ways:

(1)   Housing Benefit payments from their local Council to help with:
- rent
- council tax
- hostel charges
- some service/maintenance charges

(2)   Housing costs payments as part of their Income Support, ie:
- mortgage interest payments, subject to limit of £100,000 from 13 April 1995
- interest on loans for essential repairs and certain improvements to the home and in certain cases some loans
- ground rents (feu duty in Scotland)
- some service/maintenance charges
- co-ownership and crown tenancy charge
- charges for tents

Costs such as water charges, some repairs and insurance costs, and cesspit emptying are treated as covered by the personal allowance. The rent for a croft is now covered by the Housing Benefit scheme.

Mortgage interest payments (Leaflet IS8)

From October 1995, there is a "waiting" period for most customers before the eligible housing costs can be paid **except** for customers (or their partner) aged 60 or over who will be entitled to 100% mortgage interest from the start of their claim or the 60th birthday.

The standard interest rate (SIR) will still apply if applicable.

Existing Borrowers (loans taken out <u>before</u> 2/10/95) Form M1 12 sent after 4 weeks

- no help for the first 8 weeks

- 50% of eligible housing costs for the next 18 weeks

- 100% of eligible housing costs from 27 weeks

New Borrowers (loans taken out <u>after</u> 1/10/95) Form M1 12 sent after 36 weeks

- no help for the first 39 weeks

- 100% of eligible housing costs from 40 weeks

Exceptions

Some customers who are new borrowers will be treated as existing borrowers eg:

- those treated as a carer for IS purposes

- prisoners on remand

- those whose Mortgage Protection Policy will not pay because the claim is a result of a pre-existing medical condition

- a claim made on desertion or death of a partner and the customer has children under 18

Housing costs are payable immediately if:

- customer or partner is aged 60 or over

- are co-owners

Linking claims

If a break in claim is made for 12 weeks or less, the new claim will be treated as continuous with the previous one and the appropriate "mortgage rules" applied ie prior to or from October 1995.

In some circumstances this can be extended to 26 weeks or even indefinitely.

Mortgage payment protection policies

Some income from Mortgage payment protection policies can be ignored in an IS assessment eg:

- if part of the income is used to pay the policy itself

- the income is to meet interest payments that IS cannot meet due to a "waiting" period

Payments made direct to a lender without customer access are treated differently.

Other income from a policy may be offset against benefit.

Interest rates

The amount of interest paid is usually based on the Standard Interest Rate (SIR) less MIRAS.

This may not be the same rate as charged by the lender. However, if the rate charged by the lender is below 5% that rate is then used. If the rate is above 5%, the SIR applies and once SIR is paid it will not be removed.

Payment

If the lender participates in the Mortgage Interest Direct Scheme, payment is sent to the lender every 4 weeks. If the lender is not in the scheme, mortgage interest will be paid to the customer with their Income Support.

Treatment of income

Income is all the money that is coming in from earnings, Social Security benefits, maintenance payments and other sources, and is treated as being received on a weekly basis.

Earnings

Net earnings are taken into account, ie earnings after the payment of tax, NI contributions and half of any occupational or personal pensions payments.

Income from boarders

A fixed amount of £20.00 plus 50% of the balance of the charge is disregarded.

Income from subtenants has a disregard of £4.00 for rent (furnished or unfurnished) and a further £9.25 if heating is included.

Earnings disregard

Normal disregards

In most cases, the first £5 of earnings is disregarded. For couples, the first £5 of each partner's earnings is disregarded.

Higher disregards

The first £15 of earnings is disregarded:

(1)   if the customer is entitled to the lone parent premium

(2)   if the customer is entitled to the disability premium

(3)   in the case of a couple who are both under 60 and have both been out of work and getting Income Support for 2 years or more; or

(4)	if the customer is entitled to the carer premium, but this applies only to the carer's earnings.

For people engaged in the following occupations, the £15 disregard may apply to that income:

(1)	a part-time firefighter;

(2)	a member of the Territorial Army or the Reserve Force;

(3)	a member of the crew of a lifeboat, or someone manning or launching a lifeboat; and

(4)	an auxiliary coastguard involved in coast rescue duties.

The maximum amount of earnings that can be ignored for a couple is £15.

Child minders

If the customer or partner works as a daytime child minder in their own home, two-thirds of the gross income is ignored completely. The other third is treated as earnings.

Councillors

Councillors are paid allowances for the work they do. These allowances are:

- Basic Allowance
- Special Responsibilities Allowance
- Attendance Allowance
- Financial Loss Allowance

Each allowance attracts an expenses element. These expenses are disregarded.

Social Security benefits

Most Social Security pensions and benefits are taken fully into account.

The following benefits are ignored completely:

- Housing Benefit (and transitional payments)
- Council Tax Benefit

- Attendance Allowance (there are special rules for people in RCH/NH)

- Disability Living Allowance (there are special rules for people in RCH/NH)

- Christmas Bonus

- Constant Attendance Allowance

- War Pensioners Mobility Supplement

- Exceptionally Severe Disablement Allowance

- Severe Disablement Occupational Allowance

- any Social Fund payment

- War Widow's Special Payment

The first £10 of the following benefits is not counted:

- War Widow's or Widower's Pension

- War Disablement Pension

Charitable income

Regular charitable income has a £20 disregard.

Irregular charitable payments are treated as capital.

Maintenance payments

Maintenance payments are taken fully into account.

Capital rule

Customer and partner : the capital limit is £8000.00 (a special limit of £16000.00 applies to people in Residential/Nursing homes).

If capital is £3000.01 to £8000.00, a weekly income is assumed as follows:

Range	Assumed Income (Weekly)
£3000.00 and below	Nil
£3000.01 - £3250.00	£1
£3250.01 - £3500.00	£2
£3500.01 - £3750.00	£3
£3750.01 - £4000.00	£4
£4000.01 - £4250.00	£5
£4250.01 - £4500.00	£6
£4500.01 - £4750.00	£7
£4750.01 - £5000.00	£8
£5000.01 - £5250.00	£9
£5250.01 - £5500.00	£10
£5500.01 - £5750.00	£11
£5750.01 - £6000.00	£12 etc to £8000.00
£8000.01 +	No entitlement

Dependants

Capital £3000.00 or less - disregard in full.

Capital over £3000.00 - dependants allowance and any premium paid solely in respect of the dependant is not awarded.

Family Premium and Lone Parent Premium remain in payment.

Capital Resources

Most savings etc are taken fully into account including money saved from income to meet recurring expenses, eg fuel bills.

Almost all Social Security and Housing Benefit arrears are disregarded for 12 months.

If capital from the sale of a house is earmarked for home purchase, it is ignored for up to six months or longer in certain circumstances. Also capital which has been acquired for the purpose of essential repairs or improvements to the home is treated in the same way.

Disregarded

The following are disregarded:

- potential surrender value of life assurance policies

- value of premises occupied by an elderly or incapacitated relative or former partner who is no longer treated as a member of the same household (in certain circumstances)

- homes put up for sale are disregarded for a limited period (initially 6 months)

- if legal action being taken to recover a home from ex-partner

- if the customer has just moved into a residential care or nursing home, their home is disregarded, provided it is put up for sale (initially for 6 months)

Other help

Other help available to customers who receive Income Support include:

- free NHS eyesight test

- free NHS prescriptions

- free NHS dental treatment

- vouchers to help with the cost of glasses

- help with the cost of travelling to hospital for NHS treatment

- free milk and vitamins for pregnant women and children under 5 years old

- free or help with the cost of NHS wigs and fabric supports

- free school meals

- help with prison visits - the Assisted Prison Visits Unit will consider help towards the cost of prison visits for people in receipt of Income Support, Family Credit, Disability Working Allowance, or who hold a remission certificate, AG2 or AG3, and are close relatives of the prisoner. For further information please see form F2022.

Help may also be given from the Social Fund with expenses for a new baby, funeral expenses or other exceptional expenses.

Residential Care Homes & Nursing Homes

Introduction

Leaflet IS50 and SSCC1

From 1 April 1993 there were changes to the way people going in Residential Care Homes (RCH) and Nursing Homes (NH) are funded.

Almost all residents of RCH/NHs on 31 March 1993 remained entitled to Income Support under rules known as 'preserved rights':

(1)   for as long as that person needs care in a home;

(2)   until the person leave residential or nursing home care permanently; or

(3)   until the absence exceeds specified periods (see 'Temporary absence rules').

People who move from one registered home to another will keep their preserved rights, subject to temporary absence rules. They will also be entitled to the IS limit applicable to their new RCH/NH.

People resident in registered care homes on 31 March 1993 also have preserved rights to higher rates of benefit if:

(1)   they are not getting Income Support, eg because they are able to pay the fees themselves from capital or private income; and

(2)   they subsequently claim IS*.

* This rule does not apply to new customers in small homes for fewer than four people, only existing customers in small homes will have preserved rights.

People can retain their preserved rights until an absence exceeds the specified period (see temporary absence rules) if:

(1)   they were normally resident in a RCH/NH on 31 March 1993; and

(2)   are temporarily absent from the home on that date.

Temporary absence rules

Permanent residents can keep their preserved rights when they return to the RCH/NH, if the absence has not exceeded 13 weeks.

Temporary residents can keep their preserved rights on returning to the RCH/NH provided their absence has not exceeded 4 weeks.

Residents who become hospital in-patients can also keep their preserved rights when they return to the home, provided the period in hospital does not exceed 52 weeks.

The temporary absence rules apply whether or not the person is an

IS customer but only if they were admitted to a home before 1 April 1993.

For people in small homes, only existing IS customers have preserved rights.

Residential Allowance

Residents who were admitted to RCH/NH from 1 April 1993 and entitled to IS are paid the normal personal allowance, residential allowance and appropriate premiums as if they were living in their own home.

Residential Allowance payable as part of Income Support

The Residential Allowance is payable as part of Income Support for:

- people entering RCH or NH from 1 April 1993 who don't have preserved rights

- both permanent and temporary residents of registered homes will qualify for RA

The local authority assesses cases individually for the care element of the fees.

Residential Care and Nursing Homes National limits

Residential Care

		Limit
Elderly		£203
Very dependent elderly or blind		£234
Mentally ill (not handicapped)		£214
Mentally ill (special criteria satisfied)		£234
Drug/alcohol dependent		£214
Drud/alcohol dependent (special criteria satisfied)		£234
Mentally handicapped		£244
Physically disabled	(under pension age)	£276
	(over pension age)	£203
	(very dependent elderly)	£234
Other		£203
Special criteria satisfied		£234
Greater London increase		£38*

Nursing Care

Mentally ill	£304
Drug/alcohol dependent	£304
Mentally handicapped	£310
Terminally ill	£303
Physically disabled below pension age	£341
Physically disabled over pension age	£303
Other including elderly	£303
Greater London increase	£43*

Residential Allowance:

Greater London	£60
Elsewhere	£54

All plus £13.75 personal expenses

* Note different amounts.

Attendance Allowance - people aged 65 years and over

Attendance Allowance is taken fully into account when assessing charges for private Residential Care and Nursing homes, where the customer is receiving the higher rate of Income Support because of Preserved Rights.

Disability Living Allowance

New cases

Only the care component is taken into account when assessing charges for private Residential Care and Nursing homes.

Attendance Allowance and Disability Living Allowance care component

From 1 April 1993, customers who permanently move into a Residential Care Home or Nursing Home (RCH/NH) and who get Attendance Allowance or the Disability Living Allowance care component have these benefits withdrawn after 28 days. Attendance

Allowance is disregarded for the 28 days it is in payment. The Social Services Department adjust their payment to take account of this.

Exceptionally, if the customer is meeting the full cost of their RCH/NH fees, they will continue to receive Attendance Allowance or Disability Living Allowance care component and may therefore qualify for the Severe Disability Premium if they live alone.

Note

From April 1996, the capital limit for people in or about to enter RCH and NH will be raised to £16,000. Also the first £10,000 will be ignored for "tariff income" purposes. This will apply to Income Support, Housing Benefit and Local Authourity charging assessments.

Income Support and Social Fund

Board and Lodging

Hostels

A hostel resident eligible for Income Support may receive help with their accommodation charge through the Housing Benefits scheme (which is administered by the local council). Personal needs are met from Income Support. This is made up from the same types of basic allowances and premiums that other Income Support customers get.

Meals deductions

Full board	Adult £17.10	Children under 16 £8.65
Breakfast only	Adult £ 2.05	Children under 16 £2.05
Part board	Adult £11.35	Children under 16 £5.70

Fuel deductions

One room	£5.60
Heating and hot water	£10.40
Lighting	£0.80
Cooking (if facilities available)	£1.15

Exceptionally, if the boarder occupies more than one room, a higher deduction is made - see leaflet NI 196 for the rates.

Income Support and Social Fund

Transitional Protection

- Customers living in hostels on 9 October 1989 receive additional payments if their disposable income after meeting the hostel fee goes down.

  These payments continue for as long as the customer continues to live at the same hostel. They will be reduced only as normal benefit rates increase.

- Hostels receive additional payments from a Central Unit to make up any shortfall between the hostel charge met by Housing Benefit and the hostel charge formerly met by Income Support.

Discretionary Payments from the Social Fund

Introduction

SB16 Guide to the Social Fund

SFL 2, IRS 1

Claim form SF300

The Social fund helps people with exceptional expenses which are difficult for them to meet from their regular income.

There are 3 types of payments:

- Community Care Grants

- Budgeting Loans

- Crisis Loans

The Budget

Each District is allocated a budget at the beginning of the financial year (April - March). The budget is divided into an amount for grants and an amount for loans. It is monitored against a predicted seasonal pattern of need and will provide for some contingency arrangements for exceptional circumstances. The contingency fund is held centrally. The budget must not be exceeded within the financial year, and figures will be published.

Reviews

If an applicant disagrees with the Social Fund Officer's (SFO) decision, the applicant may ask for a review. A request for a review of the decision must be made in writing within 28 days of the issue of the decision and contain reasons for review. The Reviewing Officer will look at all the circumstances and if he is unable to change the decision wholly in the applicant's favour, the applicant will be invited to the office for an interview to explain the decision and to give the applicant the opportunity to put forward their case. If the decision cannot be changed in the applicant's favour the Reviewing Officer will consider the case and issue a decision.

If the applicant is not satisfied with the revised decision he has a further 28 days in which to apply to a Social Fund Inspector of the Independent Review Service. Inspectors are independent of the Department and are answerable to the Social Fund Commissioner. An Inspector has the power to confirm the SFO's decision, to refer the case back to the Social Fund Review Officer or to substitute his own decision.

Community Care Grants

Community Care Grants (CCG) are for people getting Income Support or who expect to get Income Support within 6 weeks of discharge from institutional or residential care. CCGs are to help people:

- remain in the community rather than enter institutional or residential care

- return to the community from institutional or residential care

- cope with very difficult problems in their family such as disability

- to help with the expenses of travel within the UK in some circumstances, eg to visit someone who is ill

- allow the applicant or his partner to care for a prisoner or young offender on home leave

Conditions

- any capital in excess of £500 must be used towards the grant, (over £1000 if customer or partner is aged 60+)

- minimum grant £30 unless the request is for fares or travelling expenses

There is no maximum amount. The Social Fund Officer must consider the priority of the claim and the state of the budget when making their decision.

The main types of help suggested are:

- start-up grants

- grants for clothing

- removal costs instead of some or all start-up grant

- fares to move home

- fuel connection charge (but not fuel bills)

Repayment

CCGs are grants and therefore not repayable.

Exclusions

The exclusions are broadly the same as for Budgeting Loans, including:

- installation, rental and call charges for a telephone

- any expenses which the Local Authority has a statutory duty to meet

- costs of fuel consumption and any associated standing charges

- housing costs, including repairs and improvements to the home which the Income Support (General) Regulations 1987 Schedule 3 paragraph 8(3) refers and including deposits to secure accommodation, mortgage payments, water rates, sewerage rates, service charges, rent and all other charges for accommodation whether or not such charges include payment for meals/and or services other than:
  - minor repairs and improvements
  - charges for accommodation applied for through the local authority

- council tax, council water charges, arrears of community charge, collective community contributions or community water charges

- any daily living expenses such as food and groceries, except:
  - where such expenses are incurred in caring for a prisoner or young offender on release on temporary licence under rule 6 of the Prison Rules 1964 or, in Scotland, on temporary release under Part XIV of the Prisons and Young Offenders Institutions (Scotland) Rules 1994
  - where a crisis loan cannot be awarded for such expenses because the maximum amount referred to in direction 18 has already been reached

Budgeting Loans

Budgeting Loans help customers who receive Income Support to spread large one-off expenses.

Conditions

- the applicant or partner must be in receipt of Income Support, <u>and</u> have been getting Income Support (or been the partner of someone getting Income Support) for 26 weeks without a break, (one break of less than 14 days does not matter)

- any savings over £500 must be used towards the item needed unless the customer or their partner is aged over 60. For customers aged 60+ or whose partner is aged 60+, any savings of over £1000 must be used

- the SFO must consider the priority of the claim and the state of the budget when making their decision

- a budgeting loan cannot be awarded in excess of the amount which the applicant is likely to repay

- minimum loan is £30   maximum loan is £1000

There is not a national price list.

Repayment period and deductions

The repayment period is normally 78 weeks. The repayment period can be extended in exceptional circumstances to 104 weeks or more. The amount of repayment will be dependent on the applicant's circumstances.

Recovery deductions can be made at any of the following rates:

- 15% of the Income Support applicable amount, excluding any housing costs

- 10% of the Income Support applicable amount if there are small debts, eg deductions for rent arrears

- 5% if the applicant has larger commitments including current fuel deductions

A higher rate of 25% can be deducted if the applicant wishes it and the Secretary of State is satisfied that he can afford it.

Deductions can be made from any of the following:

- Income Support
- Reduced Earnings Allowance
- Invalid Care Allowance
- Disability Working Allowance
- Retirement Pension Allowance
- Widow's Pension
- Severe Disablement Allowance

- Industrial Death Benefit
- Unemployment Benefit
- Maternity Allowance
- Incapacity Benefit
- Widowed Mother's

- Family Credit
- Industrial Disablement Benefit

Deductions can also be made from a partner's benefit if appropriate.

Exclusions

A Budgeting Loan may not be awarded in respect of any of the following items of expense:

- any need which occurs outside the United Kingdom

- any educational or training need including clothing and tools

- distinctive school uniform or sports clothes or equipment

- travelling expenses to or from school

- school meals and meals taken during school holidays by children who are entitled to free school meals

- items in connection with maternity or funeral needs. These are provided for under Section 138(1) (a) of the Social Security Contribution & Benefits Act 1992

- expenses in connection with court (legal) proceedings (including a community service order) such as legal fees, court fees, fines, costs, damages, subsistence or travelling expenses (other than a crisis loan for emergency travelling expenses where an applicant is stranded away from home)

- removal charges where an applicant is permanently rehoused following the imposition of a compulsory purchase order, or a redevelopment or closing order, or a compulsory exchange of tenancies, or pursuant to a housing authority's statutory duty to the homeless under the Housing Act 1985 or Part 11 of the Housing (Scotland) Act 1987

- domestic assistance and respite care

- any repair to property of anybody mentioned in section 80(1) of the Housing Act 1985 or section 61(2)(a) of the Housing (Scotland) Act 1987 and, in the case of Scotland, any repair to property of any housing trust in existence on 13 November 1953

- a medical, surgical, optical, aural or dental item or service

- work related expenses

- debts to government departments, such as National Insurance arrears and income tax debts

- investments

- the cost of mains fuel consumption and associated standing charges

- housing costs, including repairs and improvements to the home which the Income Support (General) Regulations 1987 Schedule paragraph 8(3) refers and including deposits to secure accommodation, mortgage payments, rates, water rates, sewerage rates, service charges, rent, residential charges for hostels, and all other charges for accommodation, whether or not such charges include payment for meals and/or services, other than:
  - payment for intermittent housing costs not met by Housing Benefit or Income Support or for which direct payments cannot be implemented such as for the cost of emptying cesspits or septic tanks
  - rent in advance when the landlord is not a local authority

-   where such charges are payable in advance to secure board and lodgingsaccommodation, or residential accommodation in hostels, but not any part of such charges not relating to accommodation for example meals, services or deposits
-   minor repairs and improvements

• council tax, council water charges, arrears of community charge, collective community charge contributions or community water charges

Crisis Loans

Crisis Loans are to meet expenses in an emergency or as a consequence of a disaster provided that the provision of such assistance is the only means by which serious risk to the health or safety of the person or member of the family may be prevented or the expenses are rent in advance payable to a landlord who is not a local authority (in certain circumstances).

Conditions

- age 16 or over without resources to meet short term need

- any resources available to the applicant should be taken into account, eg:
    - capital assets
    - earnings
    - benefits
    - cash in hand
    - funds in a bank or building society
    - credit facilities**
    - money available through existing loans or overdraft facilities**

** These resources are not usually taken into account for applicants who receive Income Support.

The SFO must consider the priority of the claim and the state of the budget when making their decision.

There is no minimum payment.

The maximum payment in respect of living expenses is 75% of the appropriate Personal Allowance plus the IS Personal Allowance for any children, regardless of age (but must not in any case exceed the difference between any sum already repayable to the Social Fund by the applicant and his partner and £1,000).

Repayment Period

The same rules apply as for Budgeting Loans. If a person does not receive IS, the Loan still has to be repaid.

Exclusions

The same exclusions for Budgeting Loans apply for Crisis Loans plus:

- installation, rental and call charges for a telephone

- mobility needs

- a television or radio, or a licence, aerial or rental charge for a television or radio

- holidays

- garaging, parking, purchase, and running costs of any motor vehicle except when payment is being considered for emergency travelling expenses

- housing costs, including repairs and improvements to the home which the Income Support (General) Regulations 1987 Schedule 3 paragraph 8(3) refers and including deposits to secure accommodation, mortgage payments, water rates, sewerage rates, service charges, rent and analogous charges for accommodation, other than:
  - payments for intermittent housing costs not met by housing benefit or Income Support or for which direct payments cannot be implemented such as for the cost of emptying cesspits or septic tanks
  - rent in advance where the landlord is not a local authority
  - charges for board and lodging accommodation and residential charges for hostels but not deposits whether included in the total charge or not
  - minor repairs and improvements

There are special rules for:

- students

- persons involved in trade disputes

- persons who are (or would be) treated as a person from abroad for the purpose of Income Support

A Crisis Loan cannot be awarded in excess of the amount which the applicant is likely to repay.

Cold Weather Payments

Leaflet CWP 1

Winter Warmth Helpline: 0800 289404

This is an extra payment to help with heating costs during very cold weather if the average temperature is 0° or below over 7 consecutive days (forecast or recorded).

A meteorological weather station measures the temperature in each area.

Payment is made **automatically** to customers by the Benefits Agency.

Customers must be on Income Support and receiving one of the following:

*   any Pensioner Premium

*   Disability or Severe Disability Premium

*   Disabled Child Premium

*   an amount for a child under five

Payment is £8.50 for each spell of cold weather.

Section 5 Contents

Page

Housing Benefit and Council Tax Benefit

Section
5

Housing Benefit

Introduction

Leaflets RR1, RR2 & RR3

Tax free

Housing Benefit (HB) is an income related social security benefit to help people pay their rent. It is run by local councils. HB can be paid to people who pay rent to a council or a private landlord or housing association, whether they are in work or not. People do not need to have paid NI contributions. Most full-time students are not entitled to HB. People do not have to be entitled to other Social Security benefits to get HB, but people who receive Income Support will normally qualify for the maximum amount, ie 100% of the eligible rent less any deductions for non-dependants.

Residence in Great Britain

People who have come to live temporarily in the UK (eg as a visitor, student, or to work) cannot normally get HB. This is because their admission to the UK is on the understanding that they are self-supporting and "have no recourse to public funds".

People can only get benefit if they have made the UK, the Channel Islands, the Isle of Man or the Irish Republic, their permanent home. If they have entered the UK within five years of their benefit claim, the local authority will require further information.

Income and Capital

Capital

People who have more than £16,000 in capital do not qualify for HB. Capital of up to £3,000 is ignored. For capital between £3,000 and £16,000, £1.00 per week for every £250, or part of £250, held is taken into account in calculating entitlement.

Range	Assumed income (Weekly)
£3000.00 and below	Nil
£3000.01 - £3250.00	£1
£3250.01 - £3500.00	£2
£3500.01 - £3750.00	£3
£3750.01 - £4000.00	£4
£4000.01 - £4250.00	£5
£4250.01 - £4500.00	£6
£4500.01 - £4750.00	£7
£4750.01 - £5000.00	£8
£5000.01 - £5250.00	£9
£5250.01 - £5500.00	£10
£5500.01 - £5750.00	£11
£5750.01 - £6000.00	£12
£6000.01 - £6250.00	£13
£6250.01 - £6500.00	£14
£6500.01 - £6750.00	£15
£6750.01 - £7000.00	£16
£7000.01 - £7250.00	£17
£7250.01 - £7500.00	£18
£7500.01 - £7750.00	£19
£7750.01 - £8000.00	£20 etc to £16,000
£16,000.01	No entitlement

Income

Net earnings are calculated by deducting income tax, NI contributions and half of any contribution to a personal or occupational pension scheme.

The following earnings are not usually counted:

- £5
  for a single person

- £10
  for a couple

- £15
  if entitled to the disability premium, severe disability premium or, in certain circumstances, the higher or enhanced pensioner premium or carer premium or if employed as a part-time firefighter, auxiliary coastguard or lifeboat man or as a member of a territorial or reserve force

- £25
  if a lone parent

Childcare costs of up to £60 per week per family can be offset against earnings where:

- a lone parent is working 16 hours a week or more

- couples where both work 16 hours a week or more

- one of a couple works 16 hours a week or more but the other is incapacitated

This applies where formal childcare is provided by registered childminders or day nurseries, in respect of children under 11.

Childminding undertaken at home is only treated as one third profit.

Other Income

Most Social Security benefits are taken fully into account as income except:

- Attendance Allowance

- Disability Living Allowance

- Guardians Allowance

The following amounts of weekly income will also be disregarded:

- £20

  of income from a boarder, plus half of the boarder's charge over £20

- £15

  of maintenance received, if entitled to the family premium

- £10.00

  of a War Widows Pension or War Disablement Pension (councils also havethe discretion to increase the amount of these pensions that can be ignored)

- £10.30

  the total of the premium which is payable to people who work 30 hours or more each week and receive Family Credit or Disability Working Allowance.

- £20

  of voluntary and charitable payments

- £4

  of any payment from a sub-tenant, plus £9.25 where the payment received from the sub-tenant includes an amount for heating

What Housing Benefit covers

HB can help to pay the part of the rent that a person has to pay for the accommodation they live in. If a local authority considers that accommodation is either unreasonably expensive or overlarge for a person's needs, it may restrict the amount of rent on which help can be given.

This is known as the "eligible" rent. It can cover up to 100% of rent.

Rent can include some service charges if they are accommodation related, eg:

- children's play areas

- lifts

- some wardens and other management costs

- shared cleaning

Housing Benefit cannot help with:

- mortgage interest payments

- the cost of fuel for heating, lighting and cooking, included in the rent payment

- the cost of meals included in the rent

- water charges

- some service charges for things like personal laundry and household cleaning

- ground rent and service charges for the home if the lease was originally for more than 21 years

- rates for business premises

Privately Rented Accommodation (January 1996 changes)

The Housing Benefit (General) Amendment Regulations 1995 took effect from 2/1/96 for people who rent from private landlords.

This means HB will normally only meet rents which are at or below the general rent of the area the customer lives in.

Who is affected:

- anyone making a new claim for HB from 2/1/96

- anyone who moves after 2/1/96

- anyone who has a "break" in entitlement of more than 4 weeks

- those in Registered Housing Association assured tenancies/licences not providing care or support, when the LA considers the accommodation overlarge or expensive

Exclusions:

The new rules do not apply if any of the following are satisfied:

- HB is already in payment at 2/1/96

- the tenancy started before 15/1/89

- local authority accommodation is being rented
- tenancy is with a registered charity/voluntary organisation and some level of care or support is being provided (unless overlarge or expensive)

Rent Officer's Determination

The Rent Officer will work out the general level of rent for properties and the area they are in. This is called the **local reference rent**.

The Rent Officer will also decide if the rent being asked by the landlord is reasonable. This is known as the **appropriate rent**.

The LA will then decide the **maximum rent** that can be met by HB.

Note

Under the new scheme HB must be calculated taking the Rent Officer's determinations into account. Therefore <u>no</u> protection applies to people who are sick, disabled, elderly or who have children. <u>Discretion</u> replaces the protection that used to apply to these groups under Regulation 11(3) of the Housing Benefit (General) Regulations 1987.

If exceptional hardship is evident due to a "shortfall" in the HB award, the LA may meet the difference. The LA still has to consider the budget available for these payments.

Pre-Tenancy determination

This allows the customer to decide if the property they are interested in renting is affordable to them and also advises the maximum amount of rent that can be met by HB.

The LA will send the customer an application form which will also need to be completed by the prospective landlord, so that the Rent Officer can visit the property and make a determination.

Single people under 25

From 7 October 1996, HB for some single people under 25 will be restricted to the average local rent for non self-contained accommodation.

This will also apply to under 25's who claim from the 2 January 1996, on the <u>first</u> review of their claim done after 7 Ocober 1996.

Exclusions

The following are exempt from these restrictions:

- people with the care of a child/children

- people who are not affected by the January 1996 changes eg LA and registered Housing Association tenants people who are renting from a registered charity/voluntary organisation and some

- level of care or support is being provided (unless overlarge or expensive)

- people in receipt of Housing Benefit prior to January 1996 (unless they move or have a break in their claim of more than 4 weeks)

Note: These are proposed amendments to the Housing Benefit Regulations.

Crown Tenants

For the purposes of HB, a Crown Tenant is someone renting their home from:

- a government department or

- someone managing the property for the Crown

It does not mean someone who is renting their home from the Crown Estate Commissioners.

If a crown tenant is receiving Income Support then the rent will be included in the Income Support payment.

A Crown tenant cannot get help with rent from HB although help may be available from a voluntary scheme if the particular government body who owns the property runs one. If paid separately to the council, Council Tax Benefit may be paid in the normal way.

Students

Full-time students cannot claim HB unless they are in an exempted category and special rules will apply to their claim. Students partners, who are not students themselves, can claim Housing Benefit but some of the student rules may apply to their claim.

Students may still get HB if they are:

- pensioners
- lone parents
- disabled, ie Disability/Severe Disability Premiums apply
- receiving Income Support
- one of a couple (both students) with dependant children
- solely responsible for a child boarded out to them by a local authority or voluntary organisation
- under 19 years and following a course of further education (not higher education)
- part-time students
- receiving Disabled Students Allowance because of deafness

Boarders and Subtenants

People may get help with accommodation charges from HB if they live in:

- hotels
- guest houses
- lodging houses
- similar establishments

- accommodation where the charge includes some cooked or prepared meals

Deductions from Housing Benefit

Deductions from HB are made for meals, heating, lighting, hot water and cooking included in with the rent/lodging charge.

Meals deductions

	Adult	Child under 16
Full board	£17.10	£8.65
Breakfast only	£2.05	£2.05
Part board	£11.35	£5.70

Fuel Deductions

One room:

Heating and any hot water or lighting	£5.60
Cooking	£1.15
All fuel	£6.75

More than one room:

Heating	£9.25
Hot water	£1.15
Lighting	£0.80
Cooking	£1.15
All fuel	£12.35

Non-dependants

Non-dependants are people like grown-up sons or daughters, and elderly relatives. They may affect the amount of HB paid.

Deductions are made from HB for non-dependants aged 18 and over normally living with the customer. There are currently four rates of deductions.

Higher rate deductions apply if the non-dependant is:

- doing paid work for more than 16 hours a week and

- has gross earnings of £76.00 per week or more

Lower deduction applies in all other cases except:

- a non-dependant deduction is not made if the customer or partner is:

- registered blind or treated as blind

- getting AA

- getting DLA care component at any rate

a non-dependant deduction is not made if the non-dependant is:

- a prisoner

- a patient in hospital for six weeks or more

- aged 16 or 17

- on YT

- a full-time student although a deduction may be made during summer vacation if the student is working

- under 25 and getting Income Support

Deductions for non-dependants

The rate of deduction depends on the gross income of the non-dependant.

Gross income	Deduction
Under £76	£6.00
£76.00 - £113.99	£12.00
£114.00 - £149.99	£16.00
£150 or over	£32.00
Others including non-employed	£6.00

April 1996

Benefits Information
Guide

How to claim

HB can be claimed in one of two ways:

- people claiming Income Support will get a HB claim form enclosed within their Income Support claim form. Both forms should be returned to the Social Security office who will pass the HB claim form on to the council. The council may then send a more detailed form for completion

- HB claim forms for those not getting Income Support are available from the local council.

Housing Benefit rates

The amount of HB a person receives depends on:

- the amount of rent
- the number of people in the household
- their needs as laid down by Parliament
- savings
- income

For people not getting Income Support, the council needs to know how much money they have coming in and how much they need to live on.

People's needs are set by Parliament each year and HB needs are worked out using almost the same allowances and premiums as Income Support, one exception is the Lone Parent Premium which is £11.50.

Income and capital are usually calculated in the same way as Income Support.

Calculation

If a person's income is equal to or less than their needs, they will get maximum HB.

If a person's income exceeds their needs, 65% of their excess income will have to be paid towards their rent.

How is Housing Benefit paid?

For council tenants, HB is paid by reducing the amount of rent due. This is called a rent rebate.

For rent paid to someone else, eg a housing association or private landlord, HB is normally paid by paying money to the person who is entitled to HB. The money may be paid by cheque or cash, or paid directly into an account. This is called a rent allowance.

Alternatively, payment can be made direct to a private landlord if it is considered in the customer's best interests. This is done automatically if the rent is 8 weeks or more in arrears.

If Housing Benefit is not paid on time

HB claims should be processed within 14 days of all the necessary information being available or the first payment of HB to a private tenant should be made within 14 days of receipt of a claim, subject to the customer having supplied all the necessary information. Councils must make payment on account if, through no fault of the customers, the council is unable to process the claim or pay on time.

Customer disagrees with Council's assessment

If the customer does not agree with the Council's assessment, he can ask to have his claim reviewed. To request a review the customer should write to the Council within 6 weeks of the date the Council notified him of its determination. The review will be carried out by the Council, who will either revise their determination or notify the customer why their determination should stand. If, after this review, the customer is still unhappy he can write again and ask to have the determination reviewed by a Review Board.

The customer may also request a "statement of reasons" which explains in detail how his benefit has been calculated.

Changes in circumstances

Customers are responsible for reporting all changes of circumstances direct to their local council. If Income Support is in payment but then ceases, a fresh claim must be made to the council.

Housing Benefit Extended Payment Scheme

From April 1996, a person (or their partner if they have one) who starts work or increases their hours or wages, may be able to continue to get the same amount of HB they were receiving while on Income Support, for an extra 4 weeks.

Extended payments can be made to those who have been for at least 26 weeks:

- unemployed, with or without Income Support or;

- getting Income Support as a lone parent or;

- getting Income Support as a carer or;

- getting Income Support and on a Government training scheme or;

- any combination of these

In addition:

- the customer must be aged under 60 at the time Income Support ceases **and**

- Income Support must cease because of the new job, increase in working hours or wages **and**

- the new work or increased hours or wages must be expected to last at least 5 weeks

Council Tax Benefit

Introduction

Leaflets CTB 1 and RR2

There is one Council Tax bill for each dwelling which is payable by the owner, occupier or tenant. The full bill is made up to two elements:

- a property element

- a personal element

The applicant may:

- have a partner or be single

- live alone and get a discounted bill

- be a pensioner

- be buying or renting their home

- be either in work or not

- be employed or self-employed

The applicant does not have to be a British citizen but if they have entered the UK within five years of their claim for benefit, the local authority will need further information.

They do not need to have paid contributions.

How to claim

People can claim Council Tax Benefit (CTB) at any time in any one of two ways:

(1) if they make a claim for Income Support they will get a claim form for CTB (CTB1) enclosed with the Income Support form. Both forms should be returned to the Benefits Agency office who will pass the form on to the local council; or

(2)   if they have not claimed Income Support, they should get a claim form for CTB from the local council.

Maximum Council Tax Benefit

The maximum amount of benefit available is 100% of the Council Tax bill, less any deductions for non-dependants, as appropriate.

Non-dependants

Non-dependants aged 18 and over who normally live with a customer may affect the amount of CTB paid. There are two levels of deduction.

The *higher deduction* (£2.60) applies if the non-dependant is:

•   doing paid work for 16 hours or more a week; and

•   has gross earnings of £114.00 or more per week

The *lower deduction* (£1.30) applies in all other cases except:

•   a non-deduction is not made if the customer or his or her partner is

-    registered blind or treated as blind, or

-    getting AA, or

-    getting a DLA care component

In addition:

•   a non-dependant deduction is not made if the non-dependant is:

-    getting Income Support

-    a prisoner

-    severely mentally impaired

-    over 18 but Child Benefits still in payment

-    a student nurse, an apprentice or someone who is Youth Training

-    a patient in hospital for six weeks or more

- in a residential care or nursing home
- a care worker
- a resident of a hostel or night shelter for the homeless
- a full-time student (even if they work full-time in the summer vacation)

Second Adult Rebate

A customer may still get CTB if they have to pay the Council Tax but share their home with one or more persons.

The customer who is treated as living on their own, for benefit purposes may also be able to claim a Second Adult Rebate of up to 25% of their bill if someone over 18 shares the home and:

- is not paying them rent
- is not a spouse or partner
- does not have to pay Council Tax
- has a low gross income

If a customer is entitled to Second Adult Rebate and CTB, the council will compare the two amounts of benefit and award the greater one.

Exemptions from Council Tax

The following people are exempt from the personal element of Council Tax if they meet certain conditions:

- resident hospital patients
- people who are being looked after in residential care homes, nursing homes and hostels providing a high level of care
- people who are severely mentally impaired, ie who are severely handicapped or suffer a severe brain injury
- convicted and remand prisoners, except people in prison for non-payment of fines or of the community charge, who will not be exempt

- almost all monks and nuns

- people with no home, sleeping rough

- people staying in short-stay hostels or night shelters

- certain volunteers working on low pay for charities

- 18 year olds still at school and for whom Child Benefit is payable

- 19 year olds in non advanced full-time education

- foreign diplomats and foreign service personnel

- people caring for someone with a disability, and who is nota spouse, partner or child under 18

In addition, student halls of residence and the other dwellings where all the adult residents are full-time students are exempt for the Council Tax. Therefore, most students are not liable for the Council Tax. Full-time students who are liable for the Council Tax are not eligible for main CTB unless they are in the exemption group. But students can claim Second Adult Rebate. A student's partner who has to pay Council Tax may claim on behalf of the couple.

Income and Capital

People who have more than £16,000 capital do not qualify for CTB, but could still receive a second adult rebate.

Capital is taken into account in the same way as for Housing Benefit.

How Council Tax Benefit is paid

The council deduct the amount of benefit due and send a bill for any balance.

Where this is not possible, eg if the whole bill has already been paid, the council will send a refund or may credit the customer's Council Tax account with any outstanding benefit so that future instalments may be reduced.

Change in circumstances

Customers are responsible for reporting all changes of circumstances direct to their local Council. If Income Support is in payment but ceases, a fresh claim must be made to the Council.

Council Tax Benefit Extended Payment Scheme

From April 1996, a person (or their partner if they have one) who starts work or increases their hours or wages, may be able to continue to get the same amount of CTB they were receiving while on Income Support, for an extra 4 weeks.

Extended payments can be made to those who have been for at least 26 weeks:

- unemployed, with or without Income Support or;

- getting Income Support as a lone parent or;

- getting Income Support as a carer or;

- getting Income Support and on a Government training scheme or;

- any combination of these

In addition:

- the customer must be aged under 60 at the time Income Support ceases **and**

- Income Support must cease because of the new job, increase in working hours or wages **and**

- the new work or increased hours or wages must be expected to last at least 5 weeks

Section 6 Contents

Page

NHS charges

Section
6

General Information

Introduction

Health benefits is a term used to describe the following benefits:

- free prescriptions

- remission of dental charges

- remission of charges for wigs and fabric supports

- help with optical costs

- help with hospital fares

Who qualifies

People who are receiving Disability Working Allowance and had capital of £8000 or less when Disability Working Allowance was claimed, Income Support or Family Credit automatically qualify for health benefits.

Claims from others are assessed on a basis broadly comparable with Income Support. There are no exclusions, except on capital grounds.

Either partner may claim but resources will be aggregated.

Entitlement

A Claim for health benefits must be made on claim form AG 1, signed, and sent to:

Health Benefits Division (HBD),
Sandyford House,
Newcastle NE2 1DB
Telephone: 0191 213 5000.

Income Support customers who are entitled to less than 10p a week cannot receive Income Support, but they are entitled to health benefits. Customers are asked to send their disallowance notice to the HBD, who will issue an AG 2 certifcate for full help towards their NHS costs.

If a customer appeals against a decision given by an Adjudication Officer, they should be advised that if they need help with health costs or travel costs to go to hospital for NHS treatment, they should make a separate claim urgently. They should not wait for the outcome of their Disability Working Allowance, Income Support or Family Credit claim to be settled if they disagree with the decision.

The following are taken into account when entitlement to health benefits is calculated:

- requirements

- income

- capital

When requirements are equal to or more than income, a person is entitled to full help with the cost of NHS charges.

When income is more than requirements, a person may get some help toward the cost of NHS charges. However, he/she will not get help with prescription charges.

Requirements

A person's requirements for health benefit purposes consist of an applicable amount (Income Support rules apply) plus the following housing costs:

Rent

The person's net rent less:

- any Housing Benefit in payment, and

- a standard amount for heating, cooking, hot water, lighting, and

- meals if the rent includes any of them

Council Tax

Deduct any Council Tax benefit and all discounts.

Mortgage and loans

The following are allowed:

- mortgage interest payments

- mortgage capital repayments

- insurance premiums on life assurance policies linked to a mortgage

- interest on a loan for a major repair or home improvement

Housing costs are not awarded if a person has free accommodation.

Non-dependant deductions are made in accordance with Housing Benefit rules.

Income

The calculation of a person's income for health benefit purposes follows Income Support rules.

Capital

Capital of more than £8,000 excludes entitlement to health benefits.

Capital of between £3,000.01 and £8,000.00 attracts an assumed income of £1 a week for every part of £250 held. Again, Income Support rules apply.

After a claim

When a person is entitled to full help with the cost of NHS treatment, he receives a 6 month certificate (form AG 2 which has green stripes) giving him, his partner and any dependant children full remission of NHS charges, and the full value of the appropriate optical voucher.

When a person is entitled to partial help, he will receive form AG 3 (with mauve stripes), a certificate showing how much he is required to contribute to NHS costs for himself, his partner and any dependant children.

NHS treatment is normally available to foreign nationals resident in UK (normally for at least 6 months) and "having identifiable purpose of residence", ie foreign students etc provided the GP, dentist etc will accept them for NHS treatment. Refer them to the local Family Health Services Authority if there are any difficulties in obtaining treatment.

More information

Contact the Health Benefits Division.

The assessment rules are not exactly the same as for Income Support and it is important that detailed information is sought from the HBD.

NHS Prescription Charge

Introduction

Leaflet AB 11 and P 11

Claim form AG 1

Charges are made for medicines, appliances (including dressings) and elastic hosiery supplied under the NHS by pharmacists and dispensing doctors. The charge for each prescribed item is £5.50 from 1 April 1996.

Some people are automatically exempt from payment of prescription charges because of their age, status, or on the grounds of a specified medical condition. These exemptions are set out below. Other people may claim remission from charges under the low income scheme if their income falls below a certain level.

Anyone who qualifies for free prescriptions should tick the appropriate box and sign on the back of their prescription form.

The following are automatically entitled to free prescriptions:

- a child under 16 years of age

- young people aged 16 or over but under age 19 and still in full-time education

- a man or woman aged 60 years or over

- people holding a FHSA exemption certificate (in England and Wales) or a NHS Health Board exemption certificate (in Scotland) who suffer from one of the following medical conditions:
    - diabetes mellitus except when treatment is by diet alone
    - myxoedema or other conditions where supplemental thyroid hormone is necessary
    - hypoparathyroidism
    - diabetes insipidus and other forms of hypopituitarism
    - forms of hypoadrenalism (including Addison's disease) for which specific substitution therapy is essential
    - myasthenia gravis

- epilepsy requiring continuous anti-convulsive therapy
- a continuing physical disability which prevents the patient leaving his home without the help of another person (this does not mean a temporary disability even if it is likely to last a few months)
- permanent fistula (including caecostomy, colostomy, laryngostomy or ileostomy) requiring continuous surgical dressing or an appliance <u>or</u>
- an expectant mother or a woman who has had a baby within the last 12 months

- a war or service disablement pensioner for prescriptions needed for treating his accepted war or service disablement (holding DSS exemption certificate)

- a person receiving Income Support

- a person entitled to Family Credit

- a person receiving Disability Working Allowance and had capital of £8000 or less when Disability Working Allowance was claimed

- a person holding a certificate AG 2

Low income

People on a low income (broadly similar to Income Support levels) should seek a remission certificate on claim form AG 1.

Refund of NHS prescription charges

If the patient is on a low income and pays an NHS prescription charge, they should get a refund by taking their AG 2 or evidence of Disability Working Allowance, Income Support or Family Credit to any post office together with a receipt for the prescription charge (form FP 57/ EC 57 in Scotland) within 3 months of paying the charge. An FP 57 receipt can only be obtained at the time the prescription charge was paid. It cannot be issued retrospectively.

Entitlement

A person whose income is more than his requirements will not receive help with the cost of prescription charges.

Prescription season tickets

People who require several prescriptions but are not automatically entitled to help with charges can save money by buying a "season ticket" (prepayment certificate).

Season tickets can be bought using form FP 95 to cover:

- four months, which costs £28.50 from 1 April 1996 (saves money if more than 5 items are needed in four months).

- a year, which costs £78.40 from 1 April 1996 (saves money if more than 14 items are needed in the year).

Health Benefits and Prison visits

Optical Costs

Introduction

Leaflets AB 11 and G 11

Claim form AG 1

Entitlement to a NHS sight test

Since 1 April 1989 the groups entitled to a NHS sight test have been:

- children under 16

- full-time students under 19

- customers and partners receiving Disability Working Allowance who had capital of £8000 or less when Disability Working Allowance was claimed

- customers and partners in receipt of Income Support or Family Credit

- holders of remission certificate AG 2

- the registered blind or partially sighted

- those who need certain complex lenses

- diagnoses diabetics and glaucoma sufferers

- close relatives aged 40 or over of diagnosed glaucoma sufferers

- patients of the Hospital Eye Service

Entitlement to spectacle vouchers

NHS glasses are no longer available but patients requiring new glasses may be entitled to a voucher to help pay for them. The following groups of people are entitled to a spectacle voucher:

- children under 16

- full-time students under 19

- customers or partners receiving Disability Working Allowance

- who had capital of £8000 or less when Disability Working Allowance was claimed

- customers or partners in receipt of Income Support or Family Credit

- holders of remission certificate AG 2

- those who need certain complex lenses

The value of a voucher varies according to the power and nature of the lenses. The voucher can be used at any optician, not just the one who supplied it.

Unless the prescription changes a voucher can only be given once per year when the existing glasses have suffered reasonable wear and tear.

One voucher may cover two pairs of spectacles if the patient is unable to tolerate bifocals.

VAT at 17.5% is charged on glasses.

Certificate AG 3

The amount of help, if any, will depend on how much the patient has been assessed as able to pay themselves, their private sight test fee, and the value of the voucher which matches their optical prescription. The patient's optician is the best person to advise on how much help is available.

Broadly speaking, the patient will first put their contribution towards the cost of the sight test. If the sight test costs more than an "NHS" sight test, the patient pays the excess. Anything left from the assessed contribution is used to reduce the value of the voucher.

Repair and replacement of glasses

Help can be given with repairs and replacements only when:

(1)   they are for a child under 16; or

(2)   they were prescribed and dispensed through the hospital eye service (and the consultant decides that replacement is appropriate); or

(3)   the loss or damage has occurred as a result of the patient's illness.
       (The local Family Health Services Authority must approve the repair or
       replacement first.)

Refunds

Sight tests

Refunds for sight tests can only be given when the patient claims under the Low
Income Scheme and receives either Certificate AG 2 or a Certificate AG 3 which
shows a patient contribution of £13.15 or less. In both cases patients should
return to the optician who carried out the sight test. People with certificate AG 2
should ask for form GOS (ST)A, and people with certificate AG 3 should ask for
form ST(V). Refunds can only be given if the certificate AG 2 or AG 3 is dated
within 14 days of the sight test.

Customers and Partners in receipt of Disability Working Allowance (who had
capital of £8000 or less when Disability Working Allowance was claimed) Income
Support or Family Credit must claim their free sight test at the time they have it.
No refunds are available.

Glasses

Refunds can only be given for glasses which were prescribed by a hospital. No
refunds are available for glasses prescribed by a high street optician.

No refunds are available to people who pay for their glasses at a time when they
were getting Income Support, Family Credit, or Disability Working Allowance. It
is very important that they ask for their voucher when they get their prescription.

If a Disability Working Allowance, Income Support or Family Credit claim has not
been settled, the patient should not pay for the glasses. If it is likely that there
will be a delay in settling the claim, eg an appeal has been made, it is best to
make a claim to the HBD using form AG 1 and get a low income scheme
certificate for the time being.

Health Benefits and Prison visits

Section
6

War pensioners

War pensioners who require a sight test or glasses as a result of a condition for which they receive their war pension may be able to claim back some or all of the cost of their sight test and glasses. They should send the receipt for their sight test and their voucher to:

Treatment Group
War Pensions Agency
Norcross
Blackpool FY5 3WP

NHS Dental Charges

Introduction

Leaflet AB 11 and D 11

Claim form AG 1

Free automatically for:

- under 19 in full-time education

- all under 18

- expectant mothers pregnant at the start of treatment

- women who have had a baby in the last 12 months

- customers and partners in receipt of Disability Working Allowance who had capital of £8000 or less when Disability Working Allowance was claimed

- people who hold an AG 2

- War Disablement Pensioners when the treatment is for their pensionable disability

- customers and partners in receipt of Income Support or Family Credit

Low income

People on a low income (broadly comparable with Income Support levels) should claim on form AG 1. Help may then be given for all or part of the NHS charges. Claims for refunds should be made on form AG 5 and sent to the address on the form with an NHS receipt (form AG 64), or something similar which makes it quite clear that it is for NHS treatment, within 3 months of the date on the receipt. If treatment is paid for by instalments, the three months starts from the date of the final receipt.

Entitlement

When a person's income is less than or equal to their requirements, they will receive full help with the cost of NHS dental charges.

Where someone's income exceeds their requirements, it is considered reasonable that they should save towards their NHS costs. Therefore, they are expected to contribute up to 3 times their <u>excess</u> weekly income towards their NHS charges for dental, optical and wig/fabric support costs. They will only pay the actual charge if this is less.

The maximum anyone can be asked to pay is £325 from 1 April 1996.

No charge

The following are always free:

- stopping bleeding

- repairs to dentures

- calling a dentist out of his surgery in an emergency (but the treatment will be paid for in the normal way).

- home visits if necessary.

Check-ups

A charge from 1 April 1996 of £4.12 is made for initial check-ups. Check-ups are free for the people listed in the introductory paragraph.

Note: Private dental treatment is **not** covered under the above arrangements, and refunds will not be made.

Wigs and Fabric Supports

Introduction

Leaflets AB 11 and WF 11

Claim Form AG 1

Free automatically for:

- all under 16

- under 19 in full-time education

- customers and partners on Disability Working Allowance who had capital of £8000 or less when Disability Working Allowance was claimed

- customers and partners in receipt of Income Support or Family Credit

- people who hold a remission certificate AG 2

- people who are in-patients when the wig or support is delivered

- war disablement pensioners when the wig or support is needed because of the pensionable disability

Low income

People on a low income (broadly comparable with Income Support levels) should claim on AG 1. Help may be given for all or part of the charges. Claims for refunds should be made on form AG 5 and sent to the address on the form within 3 months of paying the charge.

Entitlement

People listed above do not have to pay anything. They should tell the hospital when they are being fitted that they do not have to pay. They should take with them their remission certificate or some evidence that they are receiving Disability Working Allowance, Income Support or Family Credit.

Where somone's income exceeds their requirements, it is considered reasonable that they should save towards their NHS costs. Therefore, they are expected to contribute up to 3 times their <u>excess</u> weekly income towards their NHS charges for dental, optical and wig/fabric support costs.

Charges

Charges are standard amounts and the most anyone can be asked to pay for each item, from 1 April 1996 is:

Wigs

stock modacrylic	£ 46.00
partial human hair	£120.00
full bespoke human hair	£175.00

Fabric supports

surgical brassiere	£19.25
abdominal or spinal support	£28.30

Elastic hosiery

anklets, kneecaps, leggings and stockings	£ 5.50
elastic stockings (pair) and tights	£11.00

Fares to Hospital

Introduction

Leaflet AB 11 and H 11

Claim form AG 1

Patients and any essential escorts can get help to visit hospitals for NHS treatment and associated clinics for both in-patient and out-patient treatment. The cost of visits in any one week should be aggregated.

Conditions

Help is automatically given to:

- Income Support and Family Credit customers and their dependants

- people who live in the Highlands and Islands of Scotland or Isles of Scilly and have to travel over 30 miles (or more than 5 miles by water)

- people who have a remission certificate AG 2/AG 3

- customers and partners in receipt of Disablement Working Allowance whose savings were below £8,000 when Disability Working Allowance was claimed

Low Income

People on a low income (broadly comparable with Income Support rates) should apply on form AG 1. These claims are dealt with centrally at the Health Benefit Unit.

Entitlement

When a person's income is less or equal to his requirements, full help is given with the cost of travel to hospital.

Rate

The help given is either:

- normal public transport fares

- reasonable petrol costs only up to the cost of public transport fares. This should not be confused with "public transport rate", the amount allowed is the actual petrol cost only and not a rate per mile. Hospitals set their own rates

- reasonable contributions made to a hospital or voluntary car scheme taxi fares if there is absolutely no alternative

- The hospital decides which costs may be met. If in doubt, ask the hospital first.

Payment

NHS hospitals reimburse the patient for fares incurred in travelling to hospital. If the amount is large, the refund may not be immediate. Form AG 5 is required for refunds when there is doubt about entitlement. Send form AG 1 with form AG 5 if the patient does not already have a certificate AG 2 or AG 3.

If the treatment has been arranged through the NHS but carried out in a private hospital, the refund is made by the hospital that arranged the treatment.

War Disablement Pensioners

War Disablement Pensioners travelling to hosptial for treatment of their accepted war disablement are entitled to reimbursement of their travelling expenses under separate arrangements.

Prison visits

Introduction

Claim form AG 1 and F 2022/F2023(notes)

The Assisted Prison Visits Unit deals with all claims for prison visits. Their address is:

Assisted Prison Visits Unit
PO Box 2152
Birmingham B15 1SD
Tel: 0121 626 2797

Help is only given to people visiting their partner or a close relative.

Automatic entitlement

The following groups get automatic entitlement:

- people getting Income Support and their dependants

- people getting Family Credit and their dependants

- people getting Disability Working Allowance and their dependants

- people holding a certificate AG 2/AG 3 from the Health Benefits
  Division

Low income

People on a low income should apply on form AG 1.

Form F2022 should also be completed - this form is available from any Social Security Office.

Make sure a revised form F2022 (4/93) is completed.

Entitlement

When a person's income is less than or equal to his requirements he will receive full help with the cost of prison visits. People who already have an AG 2 certificate are entitled to full help with costs.

When the calculation results in an excess income figure (that is a person's income is more than his requirements) the excess amount is the sum the person is expected to pay towards the cost of the visit. People who already hold an AG 3 certificate are entitled to partial help with costs.

All references to prison visits have been removed from forms AG 1, AG 2 and AG 3. This does not affect a person's entitlement to claim helpas forms AG 2/ AG 3 continue to act as a "passport".

Milk Tokens and Vitamins

Introduction

Leaflet FB 8

Vitamins

Only expectant mothers and mothers with children under 5 years old who get Income Support can get vitamins from their local Health Centres.

Milk

Free milk is no longer available on the grounds of low income.

Expectant mothers and mothers with children under five who get Income Support will automatically receive milk tokens. One token is equal to 7 pints of milk.

People who get Family Credit do not receive free milk but there is an amount assumed within the Family Credit to help towards the cost of milk. They can get dried milk at specially reduced prices for babies under one year at clinics.

Families with disabled children aged between 5 and 16 who are not registered at school can get help with milk only by completing form FW 20. This form should be sent to:

WFRV
PO Box 1
Corby NN17 1GY

Approved play-groups etc can claim 1/3 pint free milk for children under 5 via local Social Services.

Section 7 Contents

Page

Widows Benefit and Funeral Payments

Section
7

Funeral Payments from the Social Fund

Introduction

Leaflet D 49

Claim form SF 200

Tax free lump sums

Conditions

The customer or their partner must be receiving Income Support, Family Credit, Housing Benefit, Council Tax Benefit (including second adult rebate) or Disability Working Allowance and:

- the customer must have good reason for taking responsibility for the funeral ie being the surviving partner, or where there is no partner a close relative. If there are one or more close relatives an ability-to-pay test may be applied.
  (If appropriate a close friend may be deemed more suitable than a close relative in some cases).

- the funeral must take place in the UK

- for customers aged under 60, savings over £500 are offset against payment

- for customers aged over 60, savings over £1000 are offset against payment, (thewidows payment of £1000 is disregarded)

- any available assets of the deceased and any insurance policies will be deducted from the amount to be paid

- contributions from other people may also be taken into account

- funeral payments will not be recovered from customers. However, if the deceased person has an estate, payment for funeral expenses will be recovered from this

Time limits

The claim must be made within three months of the date of the funeral.

Amount

There is a £500 limit on Funeral Director's fees to cover such items as:

- a simple veneered coffin

- funeral director's services

- care of and collection of the deceased

- hearse & limousine including travel

plus other items eg:

- crematorium fee

- Doctor's fee

- Ministers fee

- Organist's fee

and certain other expenses such as those in connection with religious requirements. Only reasonable costs may be met and there are limits which apply to some items.

Decisions

Social Fund decisions for funeral payments are made by an Adjudication Officer following regulations. They are subject to appeals in the usual way and payments are not constrained by the local office Social Fund budget.

Widows' Benefits

Introduction

Leaflet NP 45

Contributory taxable

The benefits due depend on the age of the widow, whether there are children under 19 (for whom Child Benefit is in payment) in the family and the contributions paid by the late husband prior to his death.

No Widows' Benefits are payable if the widow lives with a man as his wife or remarries.

Note: Rules for Widows' Benefits may be different in Scotland.

Late husband and widow both on Retirement Pension

No Widows' Benefit is payable. The wife's pension would be increased to the single person's rate, plus any graduated pension or additional pensions she has paid for herself, plus half of late husband's graduated pension and all his additional pension and increments.

All other cases

Widow's lump sum of £1000 is paid and then, if appropriate Widowed Mother's Allowance, Widow's Pension or Retirement Pension would be paid.

Widows over 60 whose husband was 65 or over and retired will not receive the lump sum payment of £1000.

If there are no children under 19 in the family and the widow is under 45, no further benefit is payable.

National Insurance

Widows who pay reduced rate contributions may continue to do so until the end of the tax year in which Widows' Benefit ceases.

Other benefits

Payment of Widows' benefits affects entitlement to other NI benefits.

One Parent Benefit is not payable in addition to a child dependency addition on Widowed Mother's Allowance.

Women widowed before 11 April 1988

Women who were widowed before 11 April 1988 receive Widows' Benefit entitlement on the basis of the arrangements that existed before that date.

Widowed Mother's Allowance

Paid after Widows' Allowance when the widow has a child for whom Child Benefit is payable. Child Dependency Increase is paid for each child. This is paid in addition to Child Benefit.

Widowed Mother's Allowance (Personal)

Paid after Widowed Mother's Allowance for widows when the youngest child is under 19 and has left school but remains at home and Child Benefit is not payable.

Widow's Pension

Paid after Widow's Allowance if widowed over 40 pre 11 April 1988 and childless or on cessation of Widowed Mother's Allowance.

Amount determined by age at relevant time, minimum rate payable at 40 pre 11 April 1988 and full rate at 50.

The above does not give details of the contribution conditions that must be satisfied before payment.

Widowed Mother's Allowance

Introduction

Leaflet NP 45

Claim form BW 1

Contributory taxable

A widow may be able to get Widowed Mother's Allowance (WMA) if her late husband has paid enough NI contributions and:

- she is receiving Child Benefit for one of her children or

- her husband was receiving Child Benefit or

- she is expecting her husband's baby

Contribution conditions

- Late husband must have paid 50 Class 1, Class 2 or Class 3 contributions before 6 April 1975 or earned wages of at least 50 times the lower earnings limit in any one tax year in the three tax years between 6 April 1975 and 5 April 1978 and paid NI contributions on those wages **or**

- earned wages of at least 52 times the lower earnings limit in any one tax year from 6 April 1978 and paid NI contributions on those wages **and**

- for allowance or pension to be paid at the full rate, late husband must have paid or been credited with contributions in a minimum number of qualifying years ie 9/10ths of his working life. If this is not satisfied, but late husband has paid for at least 25% of his working life benefit can be paid at a reduced rate. Special rules apply if late husband died from accident at work or from industrial disease.

Payment

- Widows Mother's Allowance can be paid direct into a bank or building society account every four or thirteen weeks in arrears

- by an order book, weekly in advance

Rate

Basic		£61.15
Child (only if CHB in payment)	- eldest child	£ 9.90
	- each subsequent child	£11.15

Additional Pension based on late husband's earnings since 6 April 1978 may be payable in addition to Widowed Mother's Allowance but this is reduced by any guaranteed minimum pension paid by late husband's employer.

With the introduction of the Lump Sum Widows Payment, Widowed Mother's Allowance starts on the payday on or immediately following late husband's death.

Passport

Christmas Bonus.

Widow's Pension

Introduction

Leaflet NP 45

Claim form BW 1

Contributory taxable

Widows Pension (WP) is payable from the payday on or immediately following late husband's death to widows aged 45 or over when late husband died, or following Widowed Mother's Allowance to widows aged 45 plus when Widowed Mother's Allowance ceases.

Contribution conditions

These are exactly the same as for Widowed Mother's Allowance.

Rate

Fixed by the widow's age at the time she qualifies for this benefit. Figures in brackets apply to deaths before 11 April 1988.

Widows aged	April 1995	April 1996
55 (50) plus	£58.85	£61.15
54 (49)	£54.73	£56.87
53 (48)	£50.61	£52.59
52 (47)	£46.49	£48.31
51 (46)	£42.37	£44.03
50 (45)	£38.25	£39.75
49 (44)	£34.13	£35.47
48 (43)	£30.01	£31.19
47 (42)	£25.89	£26.91
46 (41)	£21.77	£22.63
45 (40)	£17.66	£18.35
Below	Nil	Nil

These amounts are paid at a lower rate if the late husband's contributions do not cover 9/10ths of his working life.

Additional pension can be paid based on late husband's earnings since 6 April 1978.

Payment

- Widow's Pension can be paid direct into a bank or building society account for every 4 or 13 weeks in arrears
- weekly in advance by order book

National Insurance

The widow can opt to pay full rate contributions if she wishes to earn extra pension on retirement.

If a widow qualifies for a full but age related pension she will not be paid less than that amount on retirement.

Widows aged between 60 and 65 can choose to change to Retirement Pension if they wish.

When Retirement Pension is claimed a widow will inherit all of her late husband's Additional Pension and half of any Graduated Pension.

War Widow's Pension

Introduction

Leaflets

WPA 1   Notes about War Pensions

WPA 2   Notes for people getting a War Pension

WPA 3   Notes for people getting a War Pension (Overseas)

WPA 4   Notes for people not getting a War Pension

WPA 5   Notes for people not getting a War Pension (Overseas)

WPA 8   Can I claim?

WPA 9   Rates of War Pensions

Non-contributory tax free

War Pensions Helpline: 01253 858858

Conditions

War Widow's Pension may be payable if

*   the late husband's death was due to or hastened by an injury attributable to or aggravated by service in the Armed Forces or

*   the late husband was a civilian or a Civil Defence Volunteer etc and his death was the direct result of a war injury or a war service injury in the 1935-1945 war or

*   the late husband was a merchant seaman, coastguard or Naval Auxiliary and his death was directly attributable to a qualifying injury received during time of war or detention by the enemy or

*   the late husband's death was due to , or substantially hastened by an injury attributable to or aggravated by service in the Polish Forces under British Command during the 1935-1945 war in the Polish Resettlement Forces or

- the late husband was a member of the Home Guard whose death was due to or hastened by an injury attributable to or aggravated by service <u>or</u>

- the late husband was getting War Pensions Constant Attendance Allowance at the time of his death or would have been if he had not been in hospital

War Widow's Pensions are related to the late husband's rank.

How to claim

To claim a widow's pension, write to the following address giving details of the late husband's name, address and pension reference number:

War Pensions Agency
Norcross
BLACKPOOL
Lancashire FY5 3WP

A claim form will be sent to the widow.

Effect on National Insurance benefits

War Widow's Pension cannot be paid at the same time as National Insurance Widow's Pension.

Normally, NI benefits and pensions earned by the widow by paying her own contributions are payable also, eg any Category A Retirement Pension.

Allowances for War Widows

Where a widow has care of a child certain allowances may be payable on top of a basic War Widow's Pension eg:

- children's allowance

  rent allowance

Age allowances:	Age 65-69	£ 9.05 per week
	Age 70-79	£17.40 per week
	Age 80 and over	£25.90 per week

A supplementary pension of £51.71 per week is paid to War Widows whose late husbands died as a result of pre-1973 service (when MOD Service Occupational Pensions started). This is fully disregarded for Income Support, Family Credit and Housing/Council Tax benefit in addition to the normal £10 disregarded for basic War Widow's Pensions.

Note

Changes to the War Pensions legislation from July 1995 means that War Widow's Pension can be restored to War Widows whose War Widow's Pension had been withdrawn due to remarriage **and** who have subsequently been

- widowed

- divorced or

- legally separated

Section 8 Contents

Page

Retirement Pensions

Section
8

April 1996

Benefits Information
Guide

Non-Contributory Retirement Pension

Introduction

(Over 80s Pension)

Leaflet NI 184 (claim form attached)

Taxable non-contributory

Conditions

- Aged 80 or over and

- normally resident in England, Scotland or Wales at the time of claim and

- lived in UK for at least 10 years in any 20 year period after 60th birthday

- not receiving any other NI pension or benefit except Graduated Retirement Benefit, Additional Pension, or Guaranteed Minimum Pension, or their Category A B or C pension is less than Category D (over 80) rate

When to claim

Within the 4 months before 80th birthday and anytime after that date. Under no circumstances can a claim be backdated more than 12 months.

Payment

- weekly order book in advance or

- into a bank, or building society account either 4 or 13 weeks in arrears

Rate

£36.60 plus 25p Age Addition

Passport

Christmas Bonus.

Retirement Pension

Introduction

Leaflet NP 46   WRP 1

Taxable contributory

Retirement Pension Helpline: 0191 213 5000

Retirement Pension (RP) can be claimed within the 4 months before age 60 for a woman and 65 for a man and at any time after that period. It can also be paid regardless of earnings (since 1 October 1989).

Basic Pension

This is based on the contributions paid throughout a customer's working life.

For customers born on or after 5 July 1932, the working life is the period from the start of the tax year they reach age 16 until the end of the last tax year before pension age.

For people born before 5 July 1932 who were insured before 5 July 1948, the working life is the period from the start of the tax year they were 16 until the end of the last tax year before pension age.

If they were not insured on 5 July 1948 but were born before 5 July 1932, the working life starts from 6 April 1948.

"Home responsibilities protection" can be used to reduce the number of qualifying years needed in the working life to get a full or reduced pension. The number of qualifying years needed for a full pension cannnot be less than 20.

Contributions conditions

Two conditions must be satisfied:

- must have actually paid either 50 contributions (Class 1, 2 or 3) before 6 April 1975 or paid 52 x weekly lower earnings limit (LEL) in any one tax year since that date. If the tax year involved is 75/76 or 77/78 then only 50 x LEL need be paid and

- to get the 100% basic pension, 9/10ths of the years of the customer's working life must be "qualifying years". If less than 100%, pension is paid pro rata but the minimum payable is 25% (normally 9 or 10 qualifying years)

"Qualifying years" are ones when customer has paid or been credited with 52 x LEL in a tax year since 6 April 1978 or 50 x LEL between 6 April 1975 and 5 April 1978.

For earlier years from the start of "working life" up until 5 April 1975, all flat rate contributions and credits are added together and the total divided by 50 to give number of "qualifying years" in that period. Any surplus contributions 1-49 are counted as a qualifying year. The number of qualifying years worked out cannot be more than the number of years in the working life up to April 1975.

Rate

Man or woman (100% contributions)	£61.15
Dependant wife under 60	£36.60
Wife over 60 on husband's NI contributions (entitlement in own right, payable to her)	£36.60
First child	£ 9.90
Each subsequent child	£11.15

Additional Pension

This is paid to customers retiring on or after 6 April 1979 and is based on their earnings above the LEL since 6 April 1978. The amount varies according to earnings.

Widows can inherit their husband's Additional Pension and add it to any they have earned in their own right subject to the overall maximum £101.44

Graduated Pension

Based on contributions paid between 6 April 1961 and 5 April 1975 by all employees including married women with reduced liability. Employees could be contracted-out by their employers but they still paid a small amount of graduated pension.

The amounts paid were converted into "units" for every £7.50 paid by a man, £9.00 by a woman.

Maximum Units: 72 woman   = £5.72 (40 contracted-out rate = £3.18)

86 man   = £6.83 (48 contracted-out rate = £3.81)

The current value of a unit is 7.94 pence and this can be paid on its own or on top of a basic pension.

Widows can normally inherit half their husband's graduated pension in addition to any of their own.

Contracted-Out Deductions

Contracted-Out Deductions (COD) is a term which describes the deduction made from the Additional Pension of a customer who has been a member of a:

(1)   contracted-out salary related (COSR) occupational pension scheme

(2)   contracted-out money purchase (COMP) occupational pension scheme

(3)   personal pension scheme

The amount of the COD can comprise of:

- Guaranteed Minimum Pension (GMP) from membership of one or more COSR schemes and/or

- amounts treated as a GMP on account of membership of a COMP or personal pension scheme

When the customer claims Retirement Pension, their Additional Pension is worked out as if they had not been contracted-out.

If the amount of COD is more than or the same as the amount of Additional Pension, the Retirement Pension will not include any Additional Pension.

If the amount of COD is less than the amount of Additional Pension, the Retirement Pension will include the balance of the Additional Pension.

Price protection of COD

Although a customer's COD may remain at the same level, or only increased annually by up to 3%, their Additional Pension is increased annually in line with prices.

Invalidity Allowance (Transitional)

Paid on top of a basic pension to customers who received Invalidity Allowance within 8 weeks and one day of reaching pension age.

The rate is the same as the Invalidity Allowance in payment, reduced by any Additional Pension and (GMP/COD) entitlement.

Age addition

The basic pension is increased by 25p per week if the customer is 80 or over.

Passport

Qualifies a customer for Christmas Bonus (not GMP/COD).

Deferred retirement

Extra pension (increments) can be earned if a customer chooses not to take the pension at pension age or later cancels their entitlement provided they are under age 70 man or 65 woman.

Periods of deferment of less than 7 weeks do not count nor does any Sunday or a day for which a specified NI benefit is paid to the customer.

The extra pension is 1/7p per £1.00 of weekly pension for every 6 days pension is deferred.

This works out at a 1% increase for every 7 weeks or 7.5% a year, so the maximum increment that can be gained if pension is deferred for the full 5 years is just over 37%.

Special rules apply to widows and widowers.

From 2010 there will be no limit to the number of years a pension can be deferred and the increase will be rated at 10%.

Married women

Can qualify for a pension on their own or their husband's insurance.

Normal rules apply if claiming on their own insurance but if totally based on their husband's insurance, then no married womans pension is payable until he is aged 65 and claims his pension.

The husband claims a dependant's increase for women under age 60.

From 2010 a wife can claim for her husband on an equal opportunity basis for a Category B pension or on an adult dependency basis.

Earnings of adult dependant

Receiving increase before 16 September 1985.

Under £45	=	no adjustment
Between £45 and £49	=	5p reduction for every 10p earned
Over £49	=	5p reduction for 5p earned

Receiving increase after 16 September 1985

There is no increase if earnings exceed £48.25.

Dependant's Occupational Pension is treated as earnings.

Divorced persons

Special rules exist so that divorced people can use the contributions paid by their spouse prior to divorce to help them qualify for a basic pension.

Additional pension is based on the person's own contributions.

These rules apply to people divorced both under and over pension age.

Widow and Widowers

Can use their deceased partners NI record to obtain a basic pension if they cannot qualify for a full one on their own.

Reforms relating to Additional pension (SERPS)

Introduction

Leaflets CA01, CA03 and NP39

Background

The number of elderly people in the population has risen substantially over the past 5 years and will again rise rapidly at the start of the next century.

Therefore the cost of paying for basic pension and SERPS will not be met by current contribution payments.

Under the present pension arrangements the SERPS scheme has not encouraged an increase in occupational or personal pension coverage. This is considered to be partly due to the complexity of contracting-out rules. The Social Security Act 1986 sets out to reduce the cost of SERPS and encourage alternative contracted-out pension cover.

Changes to SERPS

The new maximum SERPS will be based on 20% of average lifetime earnings rather than 25% of the best 20 years as now.

The new arrangements will only affect people reaching pension age on or after 6 April 1999. The changes will be phased in gradually over the following 10 years so that people retiring after 6 April 2009 will only receive a SERPS pension of 20% of their relevant earnings.

Tax year in which pension age reached and % of total surplus earnings from 1988/89:

1999/2000	25%
2000/2001	24½%
2001/2002	24%
2002/2003	23½%
2003/2004	23%
2004/2005	22½%
2005/2006	22%
2006/2007	21½%
2008/2009	20½%
2009/2010	20%

Widows and widowers over 65 will be able to inherit up to half their partner's SERPS pension, instead of the full amount. This particular change will not happen until the year 2000.

Serps will cover HRP from 1999 to avoid average earnings being eroded by years out of employment. FC and DWA will also be counted as earnings for Serps.

People will be split into three categories:

- those reaching pension age before 6 April 1999 will have their SERPS based on current rules (25% of best 20 years)

- those reaching pension age on or after 6 April 2009 will have their pension based on 20% lifetime earnings

- those reaching pension age between 6 April 1999 and 5 April 2009 will have SERPS worked out in two parts

- pension from 78/79 to 87/88 will be multiplied by 25% and divided by the number of years between 78/79 and the tax year ending before the one in which pension age is reached

- pension from 88/89 to last complete tax year before pension age will be multiplied by a figure between 20% and 25% and divided by the number of years between 78/79 and the tax year ending before the one in which pension age is reached

Example

Man aged 65 in September 2007

Earnings will be averaged over 29 years from 1978/79 - 2006/07.

Total revalued relevant earnings 1978/79 to 1987/88   = £ 80,000

Total revalued relevant earnings 1988/89 to 2006/07   = £152,000

Pension calculation =

$$\frac{£80,000 \times 25\%}{29} \qquad \frac{£152,000 \times 21\%}{29}$$

=   £689.65 + £1,100.68

£1,790.33 ÷ 52   =   £34.42 SERPS payable.

Occupational pensions

Delaying the change in SERPS until the next century and by phasing it in over ten years has allowed people plenty of time to make additional or alternative provision if they wish.

At present employers who offer a salary related pension scheme can contract-out of SERPS. In order to do so they had to satisfy a number of very complicated conditions, which was an obvious deterrent.

The 1986 Act simplified the conditions and removes complicated tests about the relationship between pension and earnings.

From April 1988, employers can set up schemes on a contracted-out "money-purchase" basis. They are required to pay in a minimum level of contributions to a pension scheme with pension payments being based on money invested and not final earnings.

Personal pensions

Employees have the right to opt out of SERPS or their employers scheme to join a personal pension scheme.

Prior to April 1988, only insurance companies could carry out pension business. From April 1989 banks, building societies and unit trusts have been able to enter the pension market.

People who are in a contracted-out scheme pay a reduced NI contribution while employees in a Personal Pension Plan pay standard rate NI.

The difference between these two NI rates would be paid as a "minimum contribution" by the DSS direct to the PPP (including the employers contribution rates).

Additional voluntary contributions (AVC)

Employees can pay extra voluntary contributions, within tax-relief limits, into their occupational or personal pension scheme to boost their income on retirement.

Advice

People should be advised to go to an <u>independent</u> pensions advisor for advice.

The Department can only explain what the options are and advise what entitlement a person would have in the SERPS Scheme.

Equality of State Pension Age

Making the state pension age the same for men and women

The Government's proposals to bring the state pension age for men & women in line was passed in the Pensions Act 1995.

Therefore women's state pension age will be increased gradually from 60 to 65 between the years 2010 to 2020.

This means that state pension age will be equalised at 65 for both men and women from 6 April 2020.

The change from 60 to 65 for women will be phased in over a ten year period from 2010 to 2020. This means that:

-        women born before 6 April 1950 will not be affected; they will still be able to get   their state pension at 60
-        women born between 6 April 1950 and 5 April 1955 will have a state   pension age between 60 and 65 - see the table
-        women born on or after 6 April 1955 will have a sate pension at age 65

• national insurance contributions will be payable up to state pension age and would count towards both the basic and the additional earnings-related pension

Other changes

Currently, national insurance credits are awarded to men who do not work or pay national insurance between 60 and their state pension age. This is to protect their basic pension entitlement. From 2010, the arrangement would be extended to women.

Retirement Pensions

April 1996

Benefits Information
Guide

As previously mentioned, the present arrangement which allows married women to get a pension based on their husband's national insurance contributions would be extended to men. This would mean that both men and women could get a basic pension based on their wife's or husband's national insurance contributions if this were better than a pension based on their own contributions record.

Introduction of the NEW state pension age for women

For women born between April 1950 and April 1955, the following tables show when they would be able to get their state pension.

Birthdays are grouped in one-month periods. Those born towards the end of one of these periods, would have a slightly younger pension age than someone born at the beginning.

Date of birth	Pension Age (in Years/Months)	Pension Date
06.04.50 - 05.05.50	60.1 - 60.0	06.05.2010
06.05.50 - 05.06.50	60.2 - 60.1	06.07.2010
06.06.50 - 05.07.50	60.3 - 60.2	06.09.2010
06.07.50 - 05.08.50	60.4 - 60.3	06.11.2010
06.08.50 - 05.09.50	60.5 - 60.4	06.01.2011
06.09.50 - 05.10.50	60.6 - 60.5	06.03.2011
06.10.50 - 05.11.50	60.7 - 60.6	06.05.2011
06.11.50 - 05.12.50	60.8 - 60.7	06.07.2011
06.12.50 - 05.01.51	60.9 - 60.8	06.09.2011
06.01.51 - 05.02.51	60.10 - 60.9	06.11.2011
06.02.51 - 05.03.51	60.11 - 60.10	06.01.2012
06.03.51 - 05.04.51	61.0 - 60.11	06.03.2012
06.04.51 - 05.05.51	61.1 - 61.0	06.05.2012
06.05.51 - 05.06.51	61.2 - 61.1	06.07.2012
06.06.51 - 05.07.51	61.3 - 61.2	06.09.2012
06.07.51 - 05.08.51	61.4 - 61.3	06.11.2012
06.08.51 - 05.09.51	61.5 - 61.4	06.01.2013
06.09.51 - 05.10.51	61.6 - 61.5	06.03.2013
06.10.51 - 05.11.51	61.7 - 61.6	06.05.2013
06.11.51 - 05.12.51	61.8 - 61.7	06.07.2013
06.12.51 - 05.01.52	61.9 - 61.8	06.09.2013
06.01.52 - 05.02.52	61.10 - 61.9	06.11.2013

Date of Birth	Pension Age (in Years/Months)	Pension Date
06.02.52 - 05.03.52	61.11 - 61.10	06.01.2014
06.03.52 - 05.04.52	62.0 - 61.11	06.03.2014
06.04.52 - 05.05.52	62.1 - 62.0	06.05.2014
06.05.52 - 05.06.52	62.2 - 62.1	06.07.2014
06.06.52 - 05.07.52	62.3 - 62.2	06.09.2014
06.07.52 - 05.08.52	62.4 - 62.3	06.11.2014
06.08.52 - 05.09.52	62.5 - 62.4	06.01.2015
06.09.52 - 05.10.52	62.6 - 62.5	06.03.2015
06.10.52 - 05.11.52	62.7 - 62.6	06.05.2015
06.11.52 - 05.12.52	62.8 - 62.7	06.07.2015
06.12.52 - 05.01.53	62.9 - 62.8	06.09.2015
06.01.53 - 05.02.53	62.10 - 62.9	06.11.2015
06.02.53 - 05.03.53	62.11 - 62.10	06.01.2016
06.03.53 - 05.04.53	63.0 - 62.11	06.03.2016
06.04.53 - 05.05.53	63.1 - 63.0	06.05.2016
06.05.53 - 05.06.53	63.2 - 63.1	06.07.2016
06.06.53 - 05.07.53	63.3 - 63.2	06.09.2016
06.07.53 - 05.08.53	63.4 - 63.3	06.11.2016
06.08.53 - 05.09.53	63.5 - 63.4	06.01.2017
06.09.53 - 05.10.53	63.6 - 63.5	06.03.2017
06.10.53 - 05.11.53	63.7 - 63.6	06.05.2017
06.11.53 - 05.12.53	63.8 - 63.7	06.07.2017

Date of Birth	Pension Age (in Years/Months)	Pension Date
06.12.53 - 05.01.54	63.9 - 63.8	06.09.2017
06.01.54 - 05.02.54	63.10 - 63.9	06.11.2017
06.02.54 - 05.03.54	63.11 - 63.10	06.01.2018
06.03.54 - 05.04.54	64.0 - 63.11	06.03.2018
06.04.54 - 05.05.54	64.1 - 64.0	06.05.2018
06.05.54 - 05.06.54	64.2 - 64.1	06.07.2018
06.06.54 - 05.07.54	64.3 - 64.2	06.09.2018
06.07.54 - 05.08.54	64.4 - 64.3	06.11.2018
06.08.54 - 05.09.54	64.5 - 64.4	06.01.2019
06.09.54 - 05.10.54	64.6 - 64.5	06.03.2019
06.10.54 - 05.11.54	64.7 - 64.6	06.05.2019
06.11.54 - 05.12.54	64.8 - 64.7	06.07.2019
06.12.54 - 05.01.55	64.9 - 64.8	06.09.2019
06.01.55 - 05.02.55	64.10 - 64.9	06.11.2019
06.02.55 - 05.03.55	64.11 - 64.10	06.01.2020
06.03.55 - 05.04.55	65.0 - 64.11	06.03.2020
06.04.55 -	65.0 -	06.04.2020

Section 9 Contents

Page

NI contributions

Section
9

Employed Persons

Introduction

Leaflet CA01 (Employees)

CA28 (Employers)

Class 1 National Insurance Contributions

Paid by both employer and employee when there is a Contract of Service either written, verbal or implied.

Contributions are paid at a percentage (see chart).

Contributions are not payable:

(1)   by both employer and employee for:
- people under 16
- people earning below lower earnings limit (LEL) £61 (April 1996)
- visiting armed forces employees except for civilians normally resident in UK

(2)   for employees only:
- by persons over pension age

Special rules

Apply to certain groups of workers eg:

- office cleaners

- casual farmworkers

- agency workers

- part-time teachers and lecturers

- people employed by their spouse

- UK Armed Forces personnel

- Company Directors (CA44)

Employers Helpline (SSALE): 0800 393539

Note

NIC Holiday for Employers

From April 1996, employers taking on someone who has been:

- Unemployed, a Lone Parent or a Carer and getting benefit for 2 years <u>and</u>

- is in employment expected to last for at least 13 consecutive weeks

will be able to claim an amount equal to the employer's NIC for 1 year.

Changes in contribution rates and limits for 1996/97

	1995/96	Change	1996/97
Class 1 (Employment Earners) Standard Rate (for details of reduced rates for lower bands of earnings see Table A2)	2% + 10% for employees 10.2% for employers	None	2% + 10% for employees 10.2% for employers
Limits Lower Earnings Limit (LEL) *Upper Earnings Limit (UEL)	£58 a week £440 a week	£3.00 £15.00	£61 a week £455 a week
Class 2 (self-employed) rate	£5.75 a week	£0.30p	£6.05 a week
Small Earnings Exception Limit of net earnings for exception from Class 2 liability	£3,260 a year	£170	£3,430 a year
Class 3 Voluntary Contributions rate	£5.65 a week	£0.30p	£5.95 a week
Class 4 (self-employed) rate	7.3%	-1.3%	6%
Limits (Class 4) Lower limit of profits or gains Upper limit of profits or gains	£6,640 £22,880	£220 £780	£6,860 £23,660

Applies to Employee's contributions only

NI contributions

Table A2

Notes of Class 1 contributions for 1996/97

Total Weekly Earnings	Primary Contribution (Employee)					Secondary Contribution (Employer)		
	Standard Rate				Reduced Rate for Married Women and Widow Optants	Not Contracted Out Rate	Contracted Earns on first £61	Contracted Out Rate
	Not Contracted - Out Rate %		Contracted - Out Rate* %					
	Earns on First £61PW	Earns Over £61	Earns On First £61	Earns Over £61	%	%	%	%
£61 - £109.99	2%	10%	2%	8.2%	3.85	3.6	3.6	NIL
£110 - £154.99	2%	10%	2%	8.2%	3.85	5.6	5.6	2.6
£155 - £209.99	2%	10%	2%	8.2%	3.85	7.6	7.6	4.6
£210 - £455	2%	10%	2%	8.2%	3.85	10.2	10.2	7.2
Over £455	2%	(No additional Contributions Payable)				10.2	10.2	10.2

Self-Employed

Introduction

Leaflets CA03, CF 11 CA02, CA04 and FB30

Class 2 Contributions

Must be paid by all self-employed persons aged between 16 and pension age except for married women and widows with certificates of reduced liability. Gives entitlement to all NI benefits except Unemployment Benefit and Additional Pension (SERPS).

Rate

Flat rate £6.05 1996/97   Share Fishermen £7.20 1996/97

This can be paid by quarterly billing (July, October, January, April) or by direct debit from a bank account (CA04). These direct payments are collected in arrears on the 2nd Friday of each month based on the number of Sundays in the previous calendar month.

Low Earnings

Self-employed people with income below £3,430 1996/97 tax year can apply for a small earnings exception (Leaflet CA02).

This excuses them from the legal obligation to pay Class 2 contributions but does not award a credit so the exception would affect future benefit entitlement.

This exception must be applied for in advance based on anticipated earnings and can be backdated, 13 weeks from the date of claim.

NI contributions

Class 4

An additional contribution paid by self-employed of 6% on net profits between £6,860 and £23,660 pa 1996/97 tax year, collected automatically by Inland Revenue.

This payment gives no extra benefit entitlement and is not payable by people over pension age. However, it is payable by married women with reduced NI liability.

Voluntary Contributions

Introduction

Leaflet CA08

Class 3 Contributions

Paid by people not liable to pay other contributions or, paid to make up a shortfall in contributions or credits of any Class.

These contributions are only good for Retirement Pension or Widows Benefit.

Contributions can be paid up to 6 years in arrears.

Rate

£5.95 a week for 1996/97.

Home Responsibilities Protection

Introduction

Leaflet CF 411

Commenced 6 April 1978

Aim

To protect the right to Retirement Pension for certain men and women who are unable to work regularly or do some work but pay insufficient NI contributions in a tax year to make it count for pension purposes because they are required at home to care for someone.

In the case of a man his widow's right to Widows' Benefits is also protected.

Awarded for complete tax years only and protects just basic Retirement and Widow's Pension.

When you can get Home Responsibilities Protection (HRP):

Automatically awarded to:

- women receiving Child Benefit as the main payee for each complete tax year for a child under 16

- men receiving Child Benefit as above, but the man must be the legal payee (a married man needs wife's written consent that she does not want Child Benefit)

- men and women who have been receiving Income Support and not required to be available for work for the whole tax year because they are caring for an elderly or sick person at home who is in receipt of Disability Living Allowance or Attendance Allowance

Apply for HRP if:

- caring for someone for at least 35 hours per week who receives a minimum of 48 weeks in the year Attendance Allowance or Constant Attendance Allowance or the highest or middle rate of Disability Living Allowance (care component) and do not get Invalid Care Allowance

- you have been covered by a combination of conditions as above for a complete tax year

When you cannot get HRP:

- for any tax year when you are not the main payee for Child Benefit
  or

- you do not meet the other conditions already explained
  or

- as a woman or widow you had reduced liability for NI contributions. You can change to full liability by contacting your local Social Security office. New liability takes effect from the Monday following your date of claim. Full liability is irreversible.

Notes

To get a full pension, HRP should not reduce the qualifying years below 20, unless it is at least half of the years normally required. (See example in CF 411 leaflet).

It can be beneficial to pay voluntary (Class 3 contributions) if a 100% pension is unobtainable using HRP.

From 1999 HRP will be covered by Serps to avoid erosion of average earnings caused by years out of employment.

National Insurance for Married Women

Introduction

Leaflet CA13.

Some women who were married, or widowed, before 6 April 1977, mayhave chosen to pay reduced rate National Insurance Contributions.

These contributions do not count towards Maternity Allowance, Unemployment Benefit, Sickness Benefit, Incapacity Benefit or Retirement Pension. However, depending on their average earnings, women paying reduced rate may qualify for Statutory Sick or Maternity Pay.

Self-employed women who have the right to pay reduced rate are not liable to pay flat rate Class 2 contributions, although they are still liable to pay profit related Class 4 contributions. Class 3 (Voluntary) contributions cannot be paid when reduced rate has been paid for a whole tax year.

Women on lower wages may pay more on reduced rate than they would on full rate contributions.

However, before choosing to change to full rate a lower wage earner should remember that among other things:

- She cannot change back to reduced rate

- She may not pay enough full rate contributions before age 60 to earn a full pension in her own right

Any woman considering a change to full rate should read leaflet CA13 and get a Retirement Pension forecast using form BR19.

Section 10 Contents

Page

Other information

Section
10

Christmas Bonus

Introduction

Tax free lump sum payment of £10.00

No separate claim required

Conditions

The customer must be present or ordinarily resident in a qualifying country, ie:

- Great Britain

- Ireland

- Channel Islands

- Isle of Man

- EC country

and receiving one of the following benefits in the specific week - the date is announced by Parliament annually:

- Retirement Pension or Over 80 Pension

- Widow's Pension/Widowed Mother's Allowance

- Attendance Allowance

- Disability Living Allowance

- Invalid Care Allowance

- Incapacity Benefit (long term rate)

- Severe Disablement Allowance

- Income Support with Pensioner Premium, but only when the customer is over pension age 60/65

- Unemployability Supplement or Allowance, or Constant Attendance Allowance, paid with War or Industrial Disablement Pension

- War Disablement Pension, if over pension age, retired and do not get one of the other qualifying benefits

- War Widow's Pension

- Industrial Death Benefit

If the customer is not getting one of these benefits only because they are getting some other benefit, they may still get the bonus.

Payment

Most people who qualify for the bonus and are paid by order book have the bonus included in the order for the week the bonus is due.

Retirement pensioners and widows who are paid once a year have the bonus included with their annual payment.

Everyone else who qualifies receives the bonus by Girocheque, payable order or direct credit, either with their regular payment or separately.

A customer can receive an additional bonus if the partner is not entitled in their own right and both are over pension age.

Attendance Allowance (AA)

Yes   •   If the visit is temporary, AA is paid for up to six monnths.

     •   AA may be paid for longer if the customer has gone abroad for the specific purpose of getting treatment for their illness or disabling condition and their absence is still temporary.

     •   If the customer leaves Great Britain permanently AA may continue to be paid in some cases where the customer is going to another EC country

No   •   If the customer leaves Great Britain permanently, AA ceases if they are not going to another EC member country.

In either case, notify:

The Disability Benefits Unit (DBU)

Warbreck Hill

Blackpool

Lancs FY5 3AW

Council Tax Benefit (CTB)

If the absence is temporary, CTB can continue in payment for up to 13 weeks. In some cases this can be extended to 52 weeks. Confirmation should be obtained form the LA.

Child Benefit (CHB)

Yes   If the visit is temporary, CHB remains payable for up to 8 weeks. Special rules apply for longer absence, see leaflet CH6

No   If the person receiving CHB or the child for whom CHB is payable leaves Great Britain permanently, payment stops from the date of departure

Other information

Section
10

Disability Living Allowance (DLA)

Yes • If the visit is temporary, DLA may be paid for up to six months.

    • DLA may be paid for longer if the customer has gone abroad for the specific purpose of getting treatment for their illness or disabling condition and their absence is still temporary.

    • If the customer leaves Great Britain permanently DLA may continue to be paid in some cases where the customer is going to another EC country.

No • If the customer leaves Great Britain permanently, DLA ceases if they are not going to another EC member country.

In either case, notify:

The Disability Benefits Unit (DBU)
Warbreck Hill
Blackpool
Lancs FY2 0AN

Disability Working Allowance (DWA)

If DWA is already in payment, entitlement continues for the rest of the 26-week period.

Family Credit (FC)

Yes   FC remains payable to the end of the period already authorised.

Before going abroad, write about payment to:

Family Credit
Warbreck Hill
Blackpool FY2 0AX

Guardians Allowance (GA)

This is a weekly tax-free payment for a child who has lost both parents and is being cared for by another family.

GA is payable whilst abroad if the absence of the guardian or child is only temporary. Child Benefit is still payable for the child.

If the guardian or child are going abroad for more than eight weeks, or permanently, the order book must be returned to:

Child Benefit Centre
PO Box 1
Newcastle upon Tyne
NE88 1AA

Housing Benefit (HB)

If the absence is temporary, HB can continue in payment for up to 13 weeks. In some cases this can be extended to 52 weeks. Confirmation should be obtained from the LA.

Incapacity Benefit (IB) - (short term lower rate)

Yes   If the absence is temporary, the same conditions apply as for SDA.

No   If the absence is to be permanent, IB ceases unless the sickness has lasted for over 26 weeks.

Incapacity Benefit (IB) - (short term higher and long term rates)

If the absence from Great Britain is temporary, Incapacity Benefit remains in payment as long as the Secretary of State agrees that it is reasonable for benefit to be paid abroad.

If the absence is to be permanent, IB ceases unless the absence is in an EC country or certain other countries with which the UK has a reciprocal agreement.

Other information

Income Support (IS)

Yes IS may remain in payment for up to 4 weeks if the customer is not required to be available for work, eg single parent or retired

IS may remain in payment for up to 8 weeks if a child or young person is being accompanied abroad for medical treatment.

No If the customer is required to be available for work, payment ceases immediately.

In all cases contact the Benefits Agency office before leaving.

Industrial Injuries Benefit (IIDB)

If the customer is getting industrial injuries benefits and goes abroad, they can go on getting benefit as follows:

- Industrial Injuries Disablement Benefit and Industrial Death Benefit can be paid anywhere abroad at the full current amount, but you cannot get Industrial Death Benefit for a child unless the child's and/or your absence abroad is only temporary. Since 11 April 1988, Industrial Death Benefit is no longer paid for deaths which have occurred on or after that date. Widows' benefit may be paid instead.

- Constant Attendance Allowance and Exceptionally Severe Disablement Allowance can be paid for the first six months of a temporary absence abroad (and for longer in certain cases).

- Reduced Earnings Allowance can normally be paid for the first three months of temporary absence from the UK if the allowance started before the customer left and they have not gone abroad to work. It can sometimes be paid for longer than this. Reduced Earnings Allowance is not paid for industrial diseases which started, or accidents which happened, after 30 September 1990.

- Unemployability supplement may be paid for up to 26 weeks if the absence abroad is temporary. Unemploymentability supplement has been abolished for new claims from 6 April 1987.

Invalid Care Allowance (ICA)

Yes   If a customer goes abroad for a temporary absence (less than 4 weeks), ICA remains in payment. If the carer goes abroad for the specific purpose of caring for the disabled person then ICA can remain in payment, provided all the qualifying conditions remain satisfied ie Attendance Allowance/Constant Attendance Allowance/Higher or Middle Rate Disability Living Allowance remains in payment to the disabled person. Customer should contact ICA unit before going abroad.

Maternity Allowance (MA)

See Severe Disablement Allowance.

Retirement Pension (RP) and Widows Benefits (WB)

Yes   RP and WB remain in payment. If absence will be over 6 months, notify:

Overseas Group
Newcastle Upon Tyne NE98 1YX

Orders are not cashable after 3 months.

Severe Disablement Allowance (SDA) / Maternity Allowance (MA)

Yes   SDA/MA remains in payment for the first 26 weeks of temporary absence from Great Britain if:

- the customer has gone abroad to get specific treatment for incapacity which began before they left this country; or

- the customer has been sick for over 6 months and remains so for the temporary absence aboard; or

- the customer is going (for any length of time) to an EC country or certain countries with which the UK has reciprocal agreement

Special provisions exist that allow payment to continue beyond 26 weeks if the customer is:

- receiving Disability Living Allowance or Attendance Allowance; or

- a family member of a service member of the Forces

  (a) who is abroad and with who he/she is living, and

  (b) where the absence is specifically for treatment of an incapacity which began before leaving Great Britain; or

- the customer has been incapable of work for the past six months and remains so during the absence.

Statutory Maternity Pay (SMP)

Liability to pay Statutory Maternity Pay ends with the last complete week in the maternity pay period before the employee goes outside the European Economic Area.

It is the employee's responsibility to advise her employer if she goes outside the European Economic Area.

If the employee comes back into the European Economic Area thre is no liability to restart payment of Statutory Maternity Pay.

Statutory Sick Pay (SSP)

Liability to pay Statutory Sick Pay ends with the last complete week SSP was due before the employee goes outside the European Economic Area.

It is the employee's responsibility to tell you if he/she goes outside the European Economic Area.

If the employee comes back into the European Economic Area there is no liability to restart payment of Statutory Sick Pay.

Unemployment Benefit (UB)

Yes If the customer has been receiving UB in the UK for at least 4 weeks, UB remains in payment for up to 3 months while looking for work in another EC country. See leaflet UBL22. Customer should check with the Unemployment benefit office before going abroad.

No If the customer is abroad in a country outside the EC or in an EU country on holiday, payment ceases immediately.

War Pensions

War disablement pensions and war widows' pensions can usually be paid anywhere in the world. If a customer is in receipt of a war pension and intends to live permanently abroad, he/she should inform the War Pensions Agency as soon as possible at the following address:

The War Pensions Agency

Norcross

Blackpool

FY5 3WP

Additional Notes:

1. In all cases it is advisable that the relevant office be contacted before a customer leaves the country.

2. *Increases of benefit for dependants.* If a customer is entitled to any benefit abroad, an increase for an adult living with that person abroad or in the UKmay be payable. If a child's absence abroad is temporary, the customer may be entitled to an increase in benefit for that child providing they remain entitled to Child Benefit.

3. *European Community/European Economic Area.* The European Community countries are:

- Belgium

- Denmark

- France

Other information

- Germany

- Greece

- Italy

- Luxembourg

- The Netherlands

- Portugal

- Republic of Ireland

- Spain

- United Kingdom (including Gibraltar *but not the Channel Islands or the Isle of Man*)

From 1 January 1994, the countries listed below joined with the European Community countries to form the European Economic Area (EEA). The European Community Social Security rules apply to these countries as well:

- Austria

- Finland

- Iceland

- Norway

- Sweden

April 1996

Benefits Information
Guide

Other Help

Cheap travel

Buses

Most district councils run their own cheap travel schemes for pensioners and the disabled.

Trains

British Rail sell a disabled persons rail card which gives discounts to people receiving Disability Living Allowance middle or higher rates, Attendance Allowance or 80% War or Industrial Injuries pension.

Chiropody

Chiropody treatment may be obtained free at clinics, day centres or at home.

Cold Weather Payments

See Income Support and Social Fund sections

Disabled

Alterations

Social Services can help with the installation of a ramp, lift or special equipment, eg a hoist, needed in the home for convenience, comfort or safety. They may make a charge for doing this (Chronically Sick and Disabled Persons Act).

Equipment

Social Services can help with aids to assist with dressing, eating, food preparation, sitting etc.

Wheelchairs and Artificial Limbs

These are supplied by the Disablement Services Authority following recommendations from General Practitioners or hospital doctors.

Doctors

People wishing to register with a doctor or change doctors should contact their local Family Health Services Agency.

Family Fund

The Family Fund supports families caring for a severely disabled child under 16 by providing services and grants for items related to the special care of the child. These may include laundry equipment, holidays, driving lessons, clothing and bedding. The Fund cannot help with items which are the responsibility of other statutory agencies. It cannot usually help if a family's income is £17,000 or over, and/or the family has savings of £8,000 or more.

To apply for further information please write to:

Family Fund
PO Box 50
York
YO1 2ZX

Home Helps

Supplied by Local Authority Social Services Departments. A charge may be made.

Incontinence

District Health Authorities can sometimes supply free of charge incontinence pads, protective pants, sheets, nappy rolls etc.

Commodes and bed linen can be loaned by the DHA.

Legal Aid

Anyone can apply for legal aid. Whether they qualify or not depends on their financial position and whether they have a good case to fight. When the applicant sees a solicitor, he or she will advise them and say what sort of help needed.

To get legal aid income and savings must be below a certain limit. People on income support will qualify automatically on financial grounds as long as the solicitor and the legal aid board agree there is a case to fight.

Details of solicitors who offer a legal aid service can be obtained from the Citizens Advice Bureau, or the Solicitors Regional Directory (available from the local library) or in the Yellow Pages. There is a new quality scheme called franchising. Solicitors who have a legal aid franchise are especially approved by the Legal Aid Board.

Further information about how the scheme works and details on franchising can be obtained from:

Legal Aid Head Office,
85 Gray's Inn Road, London WC1X 8AA.

Maintenance Allowance

Local Education Authorities (LEAs) have the discretion to pay a means tested maintenance allowance to children staying on at school beyond compulsory school age.

Motability

A voluntary organisation designed to help people receiving the Disability Living Allowance higher rate mobility component buy, lease or hire a car, or powered wheelchair.

NHS Medical Treatment

NHS medical treatment is normally available free of charge to everyone. However, charges may be made to overseas visitors and for hospital treatment following a road traffic accident.

Orange Badges (parking concessions)

Obtained from Social Services for people receiving the Disability Living Allowance higher rate mobility component. Parking concessions for registered blind people or on health grounds may be obtained via a certificate from a General Practitioner.

Road Tax (Road Fund Licence)

Exemption from road tax can be claimed for a vehicle used solely by or for the purposes of a disabled person receiving:

* the higher rate mobility component of Disability Living Allowance (DLA); or

* War Pensioner Mobility supplement

From 13 October 1993 people receiving Attendance Allowance with mobility problems can no longer qualify. Those who already hold an exemption certificate will be protected.

Further information can be obtained from the Disability Living Allowance Unit.

School Fares

The Local Education Authority will supply free travel if the school is over 3 miles away by normal walking distance (2 miles for children under 8). This is not means tested.

School Meals

Provided free for dependants of persons receiving Income Support.

School Uniform

The Local Education Authority may help with school uniform and sports equipment if it is a requirement of the school.

Telephones

Social Services can help under the Chronically Sick and Disabled Persons Act.

Abbreviations

A

AA	Attendance Allowance
ACT	Automatic Credit Transfer
AP	Additional Pension
AVC	Additional voluntary contribution

B

BA	Benefits Agency
BEP	Business Enterprise Programme

C

CAA	Constant Attendance Allowance
CCB	Community Charge Benefit
CCG	Community Care Grant
CDA	Child Dependency Addition
CHB	Child Benefit
COD	Contracted out deduction
CTB	Council Tax Benefit

D

DHA	District Health Authority
DIG	Disablement Income Group
DLA	Disability Living Allowance
DSS	Department of Social Security
DWA	Disability Working Allowance

E

EC	European Community
ESA	Employment Services Agency
ET	Enterprise Training
EWC	Expected week of confinement

F

FC	Family credit
FHSA	Family Health Services Authority
FTE	Full time education

G

GB	Great Britain
GMP	Guaranteed minimum pension
GP	General Practitioner

H

HB	Housing Benefit
HBU	Health Benefits Unit
HM	Her Majesty's
HRP	Home Responsibilities Protection

I

ICA	Invalid Care Allowance
IS	Income Support
ILF	Independent Living Fund
IVA	Invalidity Allowance
IVB	Invalidity Benefit

J

JSA	Job Seekers Allowance

L

LEA	Local Education Authority
LEL	Lower earnings limit

M

MA	Maternity Allowance
Mob A	Mobility Allowance
MOD	Ministry of Defence

N

NH	Nursing Home
NHS	National Health Service
NI	National Insurance

O

OND	Ordinary National Diploma

P

PIE	Period of Interruption of Employment
PPP	Personal Pension Plan

Q

QW	Qualifying week

R

RA	Retirement Allowance
RCH	Residential Care Home
REA	Reduced Earnings Allowance
RITY	Relevant Income Tax Year
RP	Retirement Pension

Abbreviations

Abbreviations

S

SB	Sickness Benefit
SDA	Severe Disablement Allowance
SFO	Social Fund Officer
SMP	Statutory Maternity Pay
SS	Social Security
SSP	Statutory Sick Pay

T

TA	Territorial Army
TEC	Training Enterprise Council

U

UB	Unemployment Benefit
UBO	Unemployment Benefit Office
UK	United Kingdom
UEL	Upper earnings limit

V

VAT	Value Added Tax

W

WB	Widows Benefit
WMA	Widowed Mother's Allowance

Y

YT	Youth Training

List of current leaflets

Leaflet number	Title
AB 11	Help with NHS costs
AC 1	Take the hard work out of collecting your pension: Automatic Credit Transfer
AC 2	Now there is an easier way to get your Child Benefit
AP 1	A Helping Hand - How you can help friends or relatives with mental or physical disabilities claim the Social Security due to them
BAL 1	Have your say
CA 1	National Insurance for employees 1996/97
CA 2	National Insurance for people with small earnings from self-employment
CA 3	Class 2 and 4 National Insurance contributions for self-employed people
CA 4	National Insurance contributions, Class 2 and Class 3: direct debit the easier way to pay
CA 7	National Insurance-unpaid and late paid contributions
CA 8	National Insurance voluntary contributions
CA 9	National Insurance for widows
CA 10	National Insurance for divorced women
CA 11	National Insurance for share fishermen
CA 12	Training for further employment and your NI record
CA 13	National Insurance choices for married women
CA 23	National Insurance for mariners

List of current leaflets

Leaflet number	Title
CH 8	About Child Benefit
CH 11	One Parent Benefit
CTB 1	Help with the Council Tax
CWP 1	Extra help with heating costs when its very cold
D 11	NHS dental treatment
D 49	What to do after a death
DLA206	Disability Living Allowance payment in to a bank account or Building Society
DLA403	Disability Living Allowance/ Road Tax
DS 2	Attendance Allowance Claim Pack
DS700	Invalid Care Allowance Claim Pack
DS702	Attendance Allowance
DS703	Disability Working Allowance
DS704	Disability Living Allowance
FB 2	Which Benefit?
FB 4	Cash help while you're working
FB 5	Service families going abroad
FB 6	Retiring?
FB 8	Babies and benefits
FB 9	Unemployed?
FB 16	Sick or injured through service in the Armed Forces
FB 19	Social Security benefits - A guide for blind and partially sighted people

List of current leaflets

Leaflet number	Title
FB 22	Which benefit (foreign language)
FB 23	Young people's guide to Social Security
FB 26	Voluntary and part-time workers
FB 27	Bringing up children?
FB 28	Sick or disabled?
FB 30	Self-employed?
FB 31	Caring for someone
FB 32	Benefits after Retirement
FC 1	Family Credit Claim Pack
FC 10	Family Credit - Extra money for working people with children
FC 47	Adviser briefing
FIG 1	Social Security - Facts and figures
G 11	NHS vouchers for glasses
GLAUC 1	Free NHS sight tests for close relatives of people who have Glaucoma
H 11	NHS hospital travel costs
HB 3	Payment for people severely disabled by a vaccine
HB 4	A Guide to Disability Working Allowance
HB 5	A guide to non- contributory benefits for disabled people
HB 6	Equipment and Services for Disabled People
INF 1	Appealing against a decision
INF 2	Other help you may be entitled to

Leaflet number	Title
INF 3	Living together as husband and wife
INF 4	Changes you must tell us about
IS 1	Income Support - cash help
IS 8	Mortgage interest direct
IS 9	Direct Payments
IS 20	A Guide to Income Support
IS 26	Income Support if you are 16 or 17
IS 50	Help for people who live in Residential care Homes or Nursing Homes
NI 2	If you have an industrial disease
NI 3	If you have pneumoconiosis or byssinosis
NI 6	Industrial Injuries Disablement Benefit
NI 7	People who have worked underground in a coal mine for 20 years
NI 9	Going into hospital?
NI 12	Unemployment Benefit
NI 14	Guardian's Allowance
NI 17A	A guide to maternity benefits
NI 38	Social Security abroad
NI 92	Earning extra pension by cancelling your retirement
NI 105	Retirement pensions and widow's benefits - Payment direct into bank or building society accounts
NI 184	Over 80s Pension

List of current leaflets

Leaflet number	Title
NI 196	Social Security benefit rates
NI 207	If you think your job has made you deaf
NI 230	Unemployment Benefit and your occupational pension
NI 237	If you have asthma because of your job
NI 244	Statutory Sick Pay - check your rights
NI 246	How to appeal
NI 251	Attendance Allowance - Payment direct into bank or building society accounts
NI 252	Severe Disablement Allowance
NI 253	Ill and unable to work?
NI 259	Retirement pensions - People living in Residential Care - How you can be paid through your local authority
NI 260	A guide to reviews and appeals
NI 261	A guide to Family Credit
NP 16	National Insurance contributions for people working in the UK for embassies, consulates or overseas employers
NP 23	Employer's guide to occupational pension schemes and contracting-out
NP 27	Looking after someone at home? How to protect your pension National Insurance for employees 1994/95
NP 29	Employer's guide to Social Security Pensions Act 1975 - Procedures on termination of contracted-out employment

Leaflet number	Title	
NP 38	Your future pension - How to check your rights to additional pension	**Page** **279**
NP 39	Your additional pension statement	
NP 44	Appropriate Personal Pension schemes - A guide to DSS procedures	
NP 45	A guide to widow's benefits	
NP 46	A guide to Retirement pensions	
P11	NHS prescriptions	
PN 1	Pneumoconiosis, byssinosis and some other diseases from work before 5 July 1948	
RR 1	Housing Benefit - Help with rent and rates	
RR 2	A guide to Housing Benefit	
SA 29	Your Social Security and Pension Rights in the European Community	
SB 16	A guide to the Social Fund	
SFL 2	How the Social Fund can help you	
T1	Traveller's Guide to Health	
WPA 1	Notes about War Pensions and Allowances	
WPA 2	Notes for people getting a War Pension	
WPA 3	Notes for people getting a War Pension (overseas)	
WPA 4	Notes for people not getting a War Pension	
WPA 6	Notes for War Pensioners and War Widows going abroad	
WS1	Industrial Injuries - Supplement to Workman's Compensation	

List of current leaflets

List of current leaflets

Index

Index

G

H

I

J

Index

P

R

S

Index

Index

W

Y

Index

Printed in the United Kingdom for HMSO

Dd302306 3/96 C110 569412 10170